Common Knowledge: Living in a Human Body

By Donald Emerson Crim PhD
Patricia R. Crim BM
And
Curtis R. Crim BA

ISBN: 978-0-615-27986-2

Printed in the United States of America

First Printing

Table of Contents

INTRODUCTION………………………………..5

Chapter 1: The Conceptual Framework……..10

Chapter 2: How I came to be interested in Haptics…………………………….....20

Chapter 3: Bathroom Algorithms………….....24

Chapter 4: Kitchen Algorithms…………..…..50

Chapter 5: Voyaging the Alimentary Canal....61

Chapter 6: Algorithms VS Heuristics…..…....74

Chapter 7: Interpersonal & Intrapersonal Haptics…………………………….79

Chapter 8: The Haptics of Communication….91

Chapter 9: Haptic Theory as it Applies to Religion………………………..….97

Chapter 10: The Haptics of Musical Performance……………………105

Chapter 11: The Haptics of America and the Rest of the World……..……………….....108

Chapter 12: Summary and Conclusions…..…114

APPENDIX 1: The Haptics of Old Age..………118

APPENDIX 2: Horace Miner Quote……………119

APPENDIX 3: Why are Humans Hairless?.........122

GLOSSARY: A Haptic Lexicon......................123

SOURCES CITED....................................141

INTRODUCTION

The original title of the book is "Common Knowledge: Living in a Human Body." I chose this title because there are so many books written from the point of view of the expertise of the author. I have no problem with such books; I have read hundreds of them.

However, this project is of a different sort. The only expertise that I bring to this effort is derived from having lived in a human body for 75 years, an expertise shared with anyone who might read this essay. Another part of the background of these essays is my experiences of teaching anthropology to university students over a period of thirty-two years.

This book focuses on a core of ideas, as follows:

1. Although most conventional treatments of the human senses (sight, hearing, taste, smell, and touch) treat them equally, here we argue for the primacy of the sense of touch.

2. The sense of touch is the first to develop during the gestation period and haptic inputs are the first experiences of the developing human brain. The other senses appear at later times, and input from these is integrated into the haptic framework.

3. During the first few weeks of post-natal development, during which the other senses are now operating at full speed, the haptic inputs still overwhelmingly dominate the infant's world of experience.

4. In a different essay, I will argue that the evolutionary history of humans, during the approximately four million years that our ancestry has diverged from that of the great apes, is best understood by examining the

developments based on the sense of touch. Not only the beginnings of technology, which are based on the growing competency of the human hand, and the corresponding changes in the cerebral cortex, but also changes having to do with other surfaces of the body, such as the evolutionary loss of hair over most of the body. And even before this time period, while our entire evolutionary history was playing out, the sense of touch played a vital role. The unicellular ancestor of all animals operated primarily by the sense of touch, and gradually acquired more specialized senses which "branched off" from tactile sensations.

5. The human hand is one of the marvels of evolution. Other people have noticed this, particularly Frank Wilson, in his wonderful book, *The Hand,* in which he lays out in splendid detail the anatomy and physiology of the hand/arm/shoulder complex. My intention here is to focus on those capabilities of human hands that are accessible to virtually everyone. I will do this in terms of complexes of behaviors which are part of people's daily routines and practices.

6. Using the home as a framework, I will illustrate these manual capabilities in terms of their locations within the house. The bathroom and the kitchen will be the focus of separate chapters.

7. In terms of individual psychology, I will argue that both our subjective experiences of our selves, as well as our experience of other people, are ultimately based on haptic experience. Just as our first experience of our bodies which took place while we were in the womb consisted of haptic inputs, our first experiences with other individuals, starting with the mother, are initially and primarily haptic inputs. As we grow older, we experience people through the other senses; however, we interpret the other sensory impressions through our

framework of haptic experiences.

8. Central to our subjective life as individuals are our feelings and emotions. It is no coincidence that we use the word "feeling" to denote these intense experiences, because the term "feeling" refers to experiences on the surface of the body, as well as powerful internal states, such as sensations within the gastro-intestinal tract and appended organs. Also, we use "feelings" to describe our subjective experience of emotional states.

9. Since I have argued that our experience of both self and others is based on haptic inputs and frameworks, it follows that human social organizations are primarily devices to organize interpersonal haptics. The family, which comes close to being a human universal, has evolved as an extraordinarily stable and functional system for turning human infants into adults. Stratified social systems which organize large-scale human societies are basically devices for organizing the flow of haptic information, with the benefits flowing upward, and the penalties flowing downward. And since stable social systems inevitably involve both cooperation and competition, I will deal with these largely in terms of Comp 1 and Comp 2, as fundamental social processes.

10. The arts are also ways of organizing various channels of sensory experience in terms of their haptic contents. The underlying concept here is that of "haptic syntax". Our feelings and emotions are not simply isolated states, but are rather successions of "mini-feels" which occur in orderly, describable sequences. Each of the fine arts translates these sequences into the appropriate sensory channel, the visual, the acoustical, and the haptic. This is most transparently obvious in the area of the acoustical arts (primarily music, dance, and drama), but can also be discerned in the visual arts that produce products such as paintings, sculpture, body

decoration, interior design, and architecture. I will pay some attention to the notion of aesthetic excellence, and role played by competition in producing such excellence.

11. Human beings create objects that are both useful and aesthetically pleasing. In terms of utility, artifacts are created by human hands and further transacted, used, maintained, and ultimately disposed of by human hands. Human systems of exchange have become extraordinarily complex with the development of large-scale food producing societies, with their proliferation of technological specialists and transactors, as well as consumers.

12. Human beings are uniquely endowed with language as their major system of communication. Non-verbal communication is at least partly encoded in and transmitted by language. Chomsky has argued that since language is species-specific to human beings, it could not have evolved from precedents provided by non-verbal systems of communication among our fellow primates. I will argue that Chomsky was profoundly mistaken. Some words and phrases carry powerful haptic messages. This accounts for the universality of obscene language, as well as the use of haptic metaphors, more generally, to characterize other individuals in high-stress situations.

13. In dealing with the human body in terms of haptic experience, there are two surfaces that send haptic messages to the central nervous system. The more obvious is the exterior surface of the body, with its different regions that produce a variety of haptic sensations. The less obvious is the internal surface of the body, the gastro-intestinal (GI) tract, and its appended organs. From the point of view of topology, the human body is a torus, that is, a tall skinny doughnut, that sends

interesting signals from all parts of this tract, from the nose/mouth complex to the last six inches of the rectum, terminating with the anus. The different parts of the GI tract, in addition to their biological functions, carry a rich load of symbolism, which will be explored in parallel with the discussion of the anatomy and physiology of the body's interior.

14. An extension of this argument has to do with religion, that vast domain which seems to exist in most, if not all, human societies. The realm of the supernatural is seen as made of entities posited by us humans, constructed out of our haptic experiences, both internal and external, and reinforced by the models of other people which we use to relate to them;
and project into our internal theaters. In an important sense, these entities are our most spectacular collective artistic creations.

15. I plan to conclude with an essay which will be addressed to some of the most vexing and threatening problems and issues which we collectively face in terms of long-term survival of the human species. This may be seen as a series of footnotes to such efforts to address these problems as Jared Diamond's magisterial *Collapse,* Thomas Friedman's *The World Is Flat,* and Michael Pollan's *The Omnivore's Dilemma.*

16. Ultimately, the aim of this project is to produce a new answer to the eternal question, "What is the nature of the Human Experience?"; surely an immodest goal for the enterprise.

Chapter 1: The Conceptual Framework

Most of what you read is based on the assumption that the reader is ignorant, and the author is knowledgeable. This essay is different, in that every reader is already an expert on its contents.

Why, then, should you bother to read it, if you are already an expert on its contents? It is simply an effort to code non-verbal knowledge into verbal knowledge. We tend to distrust what we cannot know verbally.

The Human Body - An Introduction

Of all the parts of the introduction, this is probably the silliest. After all, the one thing that I can be absolutely certain of is that the reader possess a human body, which is just as familiar to her (him) as mine is to me. Is it even possible that I could have anything to say about the human body that has not been said many times over by other writers? Clearly, this is a rhetorical question, which requires a rhetorical answer, at minimum.

The only novelty about this answer lies in its point of view, which is, that the human body lies at the center of our common experiences as persons. What we know is what we experience through our bodies. Our senses provide the gateway to these common experiences. However, the senses are not of equal importance. Research has focused in major ways on sight and hearing, somewhat less on taste and smell, and relatively lightly on the combination of senses we usually gloss under the term "touch". In this discussion, this order will be reversed. I concentrate on the touch senses as having top priority, for reasons that will hopefully become increasingly clear as the discussion progresses.

The Nature of the Argument

This is an attempt to offer a new theoretical paradigm for the human sciences.
(This was written before the term "paradigm" became a mass-media cliché.)

Theoretical schemes come in a variety of delicious and not-so-delicious flavors; some are labyrinthine, closely guarded structures.

This argument is definitely on the light side, bearing a resemblance to a serious argument in the same way that a *Bloom County* sequence resembles *El Guarnica.* Structurally, it is less a fortress than a spider web, being mostly empty space, demarcated by a few, fine, two-dimensional strands. Like a spider web, it is strong on intuitive connections, and shy on substance.

The use I make of other theorists is admittedly biased and unfair (which is inevitable, as Pirsig points out). It shows a strong partisanship, as will be obvious to the reader. The good guys and the bad guys are clearly discernible by the colors of the T shirts they wear.

Concepts

Algorithms

Algorithm: Any formula consisting of a finite list of components, and a finite series of steps, either linear or ramifying, directed toward producing a desired outcome or result. The Chomskyian Finite State Grammar probably constitutes an instance. Humans are constantly engaged in writing and running algorithms, and in some societies (such as the USA), the successes and failures that people experience at running algorithms become significant sources of self-satisfaction or self-blame, with corresponding gains or losses of gumption. "Murphy's Law" represents a major codification of the frustrations individuals experience when algorithms misfire. The "algorithm" concept is derived by abstraction from our daily operations. Therefore, it is legitimate to use the same term for its source. The algorithm requires ingredients and sequential operations; it varies in complexity: the necklace (simplest) vs. the flow chart (which has the potential for unlimited complexity.)

We must strip the “algorithm” concept of its computer-like accretions.

Computer algorithms exist in the peculiar internal space of computers: binary logic, no repairs except step editing, rerunning of correction software (or hardware.) However, natural algorithms exist in real space and time: executed by human bodies (mostly hands), sometimes using artifacts or objects or substances. The framework is fuzzy logic; individual steps or operations may be repeated or repaired.

Natural algorithms are flexible, and may be altered during operation. Conditions under which they are run may shift. Most commonly, the following classes of algorithms may need to be considered:

1. Front-loading: The natural adumbrations may not get you up to the starting gate. Before you leave on your vacation, all those last-minute things cry out to be done. Usually, these fall to the woman in the party, which is why men usually complain that it takes women “forever” to get ready to go anywhere.

2. Side-loading: These are necessary sequences which need to be inserted in order to accomplish the task.

While hiking to a specific destiny, you encounter a large chasm across your path while already in sight of your goal, an obstacle which requires a long detour.

3. End-Loading: Required sequences beyond the reaching of the goal. In terms of battle, these would be "mopping-up" operations. In terms of love-making clichés, the smoking of cigarettes could be seen as an end-loading algorithm. In domestic operations, these are the putting away of tools and leftover materials, and cleanup of the work area. This is frequently left to the lower status individual, since it is assumed that little skill is required in these terminal operations.

4. Back-Loading: These are steps that must be performed in order to accomplish a task, which are totally unrelated to the task itself. If you need to go to the bathroom and accidentally drop your keys into a cinder-block foundation trying to get into the house, then getting back the keys is essential in order to reach the bathroom, yet it is unrelated to that task.

Required precursory algorithms sometimes become recursively pre-emptive in such a way that becomes a “catch-22” situation, in which every step becomes a requirement to complete another step in the algorithm. One example is if you have a problem registering your antivirus software. When calling customer support, I was informed that I would not be allowed to talk to a technician unless the registration was already complete, which I could not do without talking to a technician. These insertions may be gumption-draining (if you see yourself being victimized by these necessities), or gumption-enhancing (if you see these as opportunities to display your flexibility and ability to cope.)

Pep vs. Gumption: “Pep” simply refers to energy. A person with pep is lively, but the energy is not necessarily directed in any particular way. Gumption however, implies both motivation and energy. A person might have great motivation to do something, but not be able to because they are exhausted. For a person to have gumption, they must be motivated and also have the energy to accomplish the desired task.

Adumbrations: “Adumbrations” are more a matter of deep background, and of choosing appropriate strategies. A chef does preparations for beginning a recipe by assembling the appropriate ingredients and cooking gear. His adumbrations consist of his prior training and experiences which allow him to choose execute prep algorithms successfully.

The Operation

Each step of an algorithm must be monitored as it is being performed. Each has built in a criterion by which it may be judged to have been correctly or incorrectly executed. This not so much a manifestation of "either-or" logic so much as the existence of a threshold, a "good enough" point. The greater the stress on speed of completion, the lower the "good enough" threshold becomes (such as the well-known Murphy’s Law.)

When a step execution fails, one will repeat the step (one or more times) in order to reach the "done" point. If this doesn't get it done, then one will either invoke a repair algorithm, or engage in a repair heuristic, which will involve at least one "grope-around" instruction.

Each failure may invoke a "side-load" sequence, which may add substantially to the time and effort anticipated for the completion of the original algorithm.

Sensory Monitoring

Human beings use their brains and hands and the sense of touch for the monitoring of algorithms and heuristics. Various kinds of sensory monitors include visual monitoring, acoustical monitoring and haptic monitoring.

Visual monitoring is the most important (even among anthropologists!) it is important for some operations, but not for others (putting on makeup, yes; shaving, no!)

Acoustical monitoring includes speaking, music-making, and some technical operations (listen for the "click".)

Haptic monitoring is the most pervasive and most important (most of the bathroom routine can be done with the lights off!) Some examples of this include the following:

1. Hand-craftsmanship: acquiring the algorithms is easy, but acquiring the "feel" is a major component of mastery.

2. Cooking: the developing of the "delicate touch", from controlling the consistency of the dough to monitoring the thickness of the sauce

3. Music-making: haptic monitors in conjunction with acoustical monitors. Every instrument has its own haptic requirements, which must be painfully mastered. Brass instruments are primarily involved with the conjunction of acoustical signal-processing and haptic signals from the mouth muscles or "embouchure" the diaphragm, which initiates and controls the flow of air, (and only trivially with signals from the fingers or arm muscles) teeth, and tongue, while the string instruments involved a similar conjunction between acoustical signals and haptic signals from the fingertips and the receptors within the finger, arm, and shoulder muscles. Like the strings, the percussion instruments involve finger and hand monitors, but unlike the strings, most percussion instruments are concerned with movements

of the entire hand, and forearm, rather than just the fingers. The percussion instruments, in other words, are played with the power grip rather than the precision grip

4. Body-tending: haptic monitors predominate. Body-tending algorithms are millions of years old (shared with all other primates), while mirrors are recent. Grooming (interpersonal body-tending) involves both visual and haptic monitors.

Key Terms

In addition to being in the glossary, I am defining here some of the key terms used throughout this text. Most of these terms are used so frequently that understanding them is a must for understanding the arguments presented.

Adumbrative Behavior: A useful term from Edward Hall, denoting those acts which need to be done before beginning a task. Not to be confused with "preparations", which are the immediate pre-beginning steps. "Adumbrations" are more a matter of deep background, and of choosing appropriate strategies.

Algorithm: Any formula consisting of a finite list of components, and a finite series of steps, either linear or ramifying, directed toward producing a desired outcome or result. The Chomskyian Finite State Grammar probably constitutes an instance. Humans are constantly engaged in writing and running algorithms, and in some societies (such as the USA), the successes and failures that people experience at running algorithms become significant sources of self-satisfaction or self-blame, with corresponding gains or losses of gumption. "Murphy's Law" represents a major codification of the frustrations individuals experience when algorithms refuse to run smoothly, or refuse to run at all.

Here are some examples of algorithms:
1. Artifacts: manufacture, transaction, use, storage, maintenance, repair and disposal
2. Producing sounds and words in speaking
3. Some interpersonal encounters (conversations: from Kottak, counter encounters at MacDonald's)
4. Craftsmanship - reproduction of designs
5. Music performance - the musical manuscript - detailed, yet incomplete, in that "playing the notes" does not guarantee a satisfactory performance. Information is contained in both digital and analogue instructions (pitches and sequences are digital; meter, tempo, variable speed, and dynamics are analogue)
6. Rituals - all sorts (including ritual texts - Catholic Mass, Navajo curing ceremonies)

Artifact: Artifacts are made by human hands, usually monitored by human eyes, and by haptic signals received from the hands during crafting operations.
Coded Messages: Many human messages contain one or more messages inside (or beneath) the overt, surface message. This hidden message is sometimes referred to as the "subtext" (see Goffman, "back-channel"). The hidden message is most commonly of haptic nature, containing a judgment of the receiver as being worthy or unworthy to receive a particular message, or some other sort of haptic judgment or demand.

Gumption: From Robert Pirsig; a dimension of living and performance which makes it possible to be successful at accomplishing a goal or set of goals. (See GUMPTION RESERVOIR in the Glossary) In terms of haptics, we fall into gumption traps in the course of running algorithms or executing heuristics.

Haptic: The central concept of this entire argument. It refers to that bundle of sensations generally identified with the sense of touch, but includes sensations internal to the body, as well as external. In its extended sense, it accounts for the human ability to create and manipulate symbols, to perceive and define each other, and to create and manage interpersonal systems of relationship. It also adds a new dimension to the discussion of primate evolution.

Heuristic: A heuristic is any bundle of strategies designed to produce a desired outcome or result. Unlike the algorithm, the heuristic cannot be represented by the formal limitation set given above. Generally, heuristics are larger patterns of organized behavior, and may include more than one actor, and/or devices such as a random number generator which violate the algorithmic requirements of finiteness or sequentiality. Heuristics may contain one or more algorithms, frequently as options or subroutines. The Heuristic is any goal-directed activity NOT entirely reducible to an algorithm. It contains instructions such as:
1. "Mess around with it until it looks right."
2. "Prowl around the woods until you find the rabbit."
3. "Keep talking until the other party agrees with you."
4. "If that doesn't work, try something else."
5. "Season to taste"
6. "Pray that God will have mercy on your soul!"
Examples of heuristics include:
1. Hunting (land-based, mobile animal) [target-shooting is algorithmic; hunting is heuristic]
2. Becoming an virtuoso pianist (or any other kind of artistic mastery) [playing scales is algorithmic; playing a concerto superbly is heuristic]
3. All athletic contests - viz., Super Bowl
4. A poker game and all other games of chance
5. Prospecting for gold
6. Most conversations (except for ritual and stereotyped exchanges)
7. All courtship
8. Getting a job

9. Living to a ripe old age
10. Acing a course

Pep: Hardly a technical term, yet it takes on new dimensions when used in contrast with "gumption" (q.v.) It refers simply to physical energy; its creation within the body, and its expenditure in activity. Gumption and pep tend generally to vary together: however, a number of examples will be adduced later which will indicate that this is not always the case.

Chapter 2: How I came to be interested in Haptics

In this essay, I want to deal with the question of how I came to be interested in the general topic of Haptics (senses of touch).

In the 1950's, while I was an undergraduate at Ohio State University, I became interested in anthropology as a major. On the basis of a few introductory courses, I realized that there was a discontinuity between different parts of the field. On one hand, there was the sub-discipline of physical anthropology, which dealt with primate evolution and biological variations in populations of living humans. On the other, there was the domain of culture which contained cultural anthropology, prehistoric archaeology, and linguistics. I was bothered by the fact that biological anthropologists view the human condition as being unitary, while cultural anthropologists focus on the endless diversity, human experiences as opposed to the Human Experience.

In the early 1960's, as I was beginning my years of teaching anthropology at Colorado State University, I read a number of books and articles which address themselves in one way and another, to this problem. The work of Edward Hall on Proxemics, dealt with the ways human beings moved in space in relation to their various settings, and to each other. Ray Birdwhistell wrote extensively about the culturally specific mappings of the body. Ashley Montague investigated the sense of touch, arguing that it has been systematically neglected in favor of the more interesting channels of sight and sound. The work of Charles Hockett and Robert Ascher, in their article *The Human Revolution,* significantly broadened the discussion of the origin and evolution of language by comparing human language to other systems of animal communication. A less reputable source, which I found very useful, was Eric Berne's *Games People Play*.

At that time, a colleague named Stanley Rhine and I wrote a paper on the sense of touch and its importance in the social life of primates. This suggested to me that the origins of language were probably intimately tied to the growing and developing haptic senses of our ancestors, which were accelerated by their gradual loss of hair over most surfaces of the body.

During the middle 1970's, I had reorganized my introductory anthropology course to focus on the sense of touch and its ramifications. In reading Marvin Harris' book *The Nature of Cultural Things,* I was fascinated by his account of the way his wife prepared supper in the evening. Harris has to invent a new vocabulary to describe these behaviors, and came up with an elaborate syntax of individual movements of the hand. Harris, however, did not focus on the sense of touch, and seemed to drift off into unproductive areas of discussion. I began to try to develop some labels for these behavioral sequences that Harris talked about, and came up with the terms "algorithm" and "heuristic". I had originally encountered the term "algorithm" in one of Charles Hockett's linguistics courses at Cornell University, but used in a rather different sense. The term "heuristic" I first encountered in the appendix of Thomas Gladwin's *East is a Big Bird.* Gladwin used the term to characterize the mental processes by which a cab driver in New York City finds his way around to various destinations. As I redefined these terms, I use "algorithm" to characterize all of those operations performed by human beings which consist of a finite number of steps in sequential order. Heuristics, on the other hand, is used by me to classify those operations which cannot be reduced to algorithms. Thus, brushing your teeth, constructing a sentence, preparing a dish of rabbit stew, ordering a meal at McDonald's, and praying the Lord's Prayer, are all algorithmic in nature. On the other hand, courting a woman, composing a piece of music, creating a painting or sculpture, or making a pun (or other forms of word play), are heuristic in nature.

These things converged in my first formal essay, entitled *Bathroom Algorithms,* in which I took Ralph Linton's brief description of the way the average American male shaves his face in his book *The Study of Man,* and Horace Miner's satirical article *Body Ritual Among the Nacirema,* and extended their treatments of bathroom behavior. In this discussion, I catalog the various behaviors that a man performs in the bathroom in the morning. This turns out to be a catalog of a series of stereotyped algorithms, with editorial comments and (allegedly) amusing asides. I have not submitted this article for publication, although I have revised it on various occasions.

The general strategy appears to be useful to apply to other areas of the house with their nested algorithms. The kitchen, for culinary algorithms, the workshop, for technological algorithms, the garage for automotive algorithms, the bedroom, for those algorithms associated with dressing and undressing, and falling asleep, may all be represented by the appropriate set of algorithms.

During the 1980's, I began thinking about the question of the personality and the problems that psychologists have had in trying to reach a consensus on the definition of this term. In terms of what I was then calling "Haptic Theory", I began to think of the human personality as an input-output matrix of haptic information. Basically, it goes back to the Beatles, "And in the end, the love your take is equal to the love you make." This in turn, suggests that we can characterize people briefly but pointedly in terms of their communications. Cartoonists have known this for a long time. Charlie Brown and his friends in *Peanuts,* are clear examples of Pain-Bearers (Charlie Brown), Pain-Dumpers (Lucy Van Pelt), the Free Soul (Snoopy, who is totally unaffected by bad strokes from outside), the Artist (Schroeder, whose internal reality is so bound up in his music that he easily brushes aside Lucy's endeavor's to hurt his feelings.)

Another component of people's awareness is what we call the Self-Stoker. This component of the personality begins to develop in infancy, when the child, having gained control of its hands, begins to explore her own body. As one grows older, the self-exploration segues into an internal dialogue in which one is both the subject and the object of verbal messages, similar to the external physical messages of infancy. According to this argument, this is not psychotic behavior, but rather a normal part of everyone's self-awareness. Of course some people tend to cordon off certain portions of this mechanism, and come to regard it as coming from an outside source. At this point, it does become psychotic. One of my favorite examples of this is what I call the "Dipshit Message", which always begins, "Dipshit, you screwed up in the following way: <fill in the blank from your own experience>", and if there are people who don't have this experience, then I feel sorry for them.

CHAPTER 3: Bathroom Algorithms

"Our solid American citizen.....slips into his moccasins, invented by Indians of the Eastern woodland, and goes to the bathroom, whose fixtures are a mixture of European and American inventions, both of recent date. He takes off his pajamas, a garment invented in India, and washes with soap, invented by the ancient Gauls. He then shaves a masochistic rite which seems to have been derived from either Sumer or ancient Egypt." (Linton, 1936, 326)

* * * * * * *

"The fundamental belief underlying the whole system (of Nacirema culture) appears to be that the human body is ugly and that its natural tendency is to debility and disease. Incarcerated in such a body, Man's only hope is to avert these characteristics through the use of the powerful influences of ritual and ceremony. Every household has one or more shrines devoted to this purpose......

"The focal point of the shrine is a box or chest which is built into the wall..... "Beneath the charm-box is a small font. Each day every member of the family, in succession, enters the shrine room, bows his head before the shrine box, and mingles different sorts of holy water in the font, and proceeds with a brief rite of ablution.....

"The daily ritual performed by everyone includes a mouth-rite. Despite the fact that these people are so punctilious about the care of the mouth, this rite involves a practice which strikes the uninitiated stranger as revolting. It was reported to me that the ritual consists of inserting a small bundle of hog hairs into the mouth, along with certain magical powders, and then moving the bundle in a highly formalized series of gestures."

(Miner, 1956, 503-7)

* * * * *

The two foregoing quotes, well-known to at least two generations of anthropologists, and beloved of writers of introductory anthropology textbooks, have in common their setting, the American bathroom, and the activities which take place in it.

Now, it is clear that both Linton and Miner were pursuing the cultural uniqueness theme, and trying successfully to bring an anthropological perspective to the consideration of urban, middle-class American culture. It is also clear that the tone of both passages is a humorous one. And yet, body self-service is clearly a necessary part of any and all human cultures, following from the common-sense observation that all humans have bodies that require frequent and regular servicing, within the culturally specific codes which specify the appropriate parameters of such self-servicing.

The intention of this essay is not the pursuit of the universal aspects of body self-service (to be considered elsewhere) but rather, to examine in detail these activities in the original setting proposed by Linton and Miner. Since I have not even attempted to survey a significant number of informants at this stage of the game, I plan to use only one, myself, as a reasonably well-informed informant. In addition, I have no intention of offering a finger-exercise in ethnographic trivia, but rather, to use this as an illustration of a somewhat novel approach to the serious ask of ethnographic description.

This approach is organized around a fundamental assumption and two pairs of organizing concepts.[i]

The fundamental assumption is that we, as anthropologists, have tended to neglect the importance of the haptic sense,[2] and with it, the significance of the hands as perceivers of significant phenomena. In various ways, anthropologists have dealt extensively with at least certain aspects of hands as manipulators, although to my knowledge, no one has looked at the intimate relationship between manual perception and manipulation. And while this discussion will focus primarily on manual perception, it is also obvious that we process haptic information over the entire surfaces of our bodies. A detailed argument for this position will be reserved for another occasion.

The first pair of organizing concepts is that of "algorithm" and "heuristic". An algorithm, within this discussion, is to be understood as any human activity which can be represented as a linear or multiple branching sequences of simple operations. These may involve hands, mouths, or feet, although they may be monitored by all of the sensory channels. It seems that much is known about visual and auditory monitoring, while less is known about haptic monitoring. Any culture may be viewed as a vast inventory of algorithms, the software of that particular cultural system. Algorithms are not limited to technological operations, but are found in speech, in social interaction, and in ritual, among other arenas of behavior.

By contrast a "heuristic" may be defined as a discovery procedure, a way of dealing with a human problem or goal for which no adequate algorithm exists. Heuristics are usually more complex that algorithms, and may involve the systematic application (either by mental simulation or actual performance) of a number of available algorithms, in the endeavor to find one or combination of ones that "do the job". Alternatively, a heuristic may involve one or more episodes of apparently random "thrashing about wildly", or "riding off in all directions".

The second pair of working concepts is the distinction between "pep" and "gumption". Both of these homely, non-technical terms have been in common usage for a good long time; it took Robert Pirsig to give "gumption" a new and exciting twist. In Zen and the Art of Motorcycle Maintenance, Pirsig, in the context of trying to cope with snags in the process of repairing his motorcycle, offers the notion that "gumption" can refer to that positive mental energy that can be lost in a brief moment when a repair fails to go as planned, especially when a small, insignificant part refuses to allow itself to be removed, in order that the rest of the program can be executed (1974, 273-281).

And although there is certainly an amusing tone to this section of the book, I choose to believe that Pirsig is quite serious in intent, as he tries to fathom the fine structure of the execution of these technical algorithms, particularly when they misfire. In addition, it is also clear that Pirsig is not talking about physical energy, since it is possible (and even likely) that gumption can be lost when the body is motionless.

I intend to both broaden and sharpen this concept; broadening it to include reference to the execution of all algorithms rather than only the technical ones, and sharpening it by contrasting it with another homely, pithy term, "pep", which refers to the physical energy which is inevitably expended in the execution of an algorithm. Now, I realize that this is a deliberate simplification of the process, that I am ignoring considerations such as skill and knowledge which are undeniably part of the performance of any algorithm (especially those which require them). However, this is intended to be a "bare bones" argument, to be extended and fine-tuned at a later time. Also, this particular set of bathroom algorithms do not require anything special in the way of physical skills or specialized knowledge; it is their very banality that recommends them to our attention.

Mention must also be made of the inspiration provided by Marvin Harris. In his early, somewhat obscure little volume, The Nature of Cultural Things. Harris presents a description of his wife executing a portion of a sequence of events involved in preparing a meal (1964, 72-3). Harris, in choosing so homely an example, provides a useful precedent for the body of this essay, as well as demonstrating that domestic algorithms are localized within particular settings, taking advantage of the artifacts available in such settings.

Beyond this one example, Harris points the way to a well-thought-out framework for describing what he refers to as "cultural things", and develops a somewhat ponderous terminological system for describing these phenomena. By and large, this is admirable endeavor, although not widely emulated, and clearly maps the way to more effective ethnographic description.

Casson's detailed summary of the use of schemata in cognitive anthropology provides a point of articulation between this essay and work being carried out elsewhere in anthropology and other social sciences. In addition to fitting into what Casson calls "cultural schemata", "algorithms", as used here, would appear to fall more specifically in what he calls "event schemata", although from his examples, it seems that the algorithms presented in this discussion contain a somewhat finer texture, and are possibly richer in information (Casson, 1983.)

What I am attempting here is an extension of Harris's

original work, differing from his perspective primarily in looking at typical behavioral sequences not from the position of the outside observer, but rather, from the viewpoint of the actor.[3] One consequence of this is that I place major importance of the intent of the actor, in that I am assuming that the algorithms which are manifest in the bathroom sequence are deliberately chosen, are monitored closely during execution, and are ultimately judged as successful or unsuccessful by the actor. In addition, my scoring of this sequence implies a language track, which is mostly internal and silent, but which plays a major part in the evaluative and monitoring functions, and which may become overt and even noisily obscene when a major breakdown in execution occurs (cutting the face while shaving, falling in the shower, dropping the toothbrush into the commode, etc.)

THE BATHROOM ALGORITHMS

Setting

This particular bathroom is a scant 4 1/2 by 5 feet in floor space, with about 50% of this taken up by the shower-tub stall. In addition, it is equipped with a wash basin with a mirrored cabinet above it, and a commode. There is a second cabinet built into the wall to the left of the basin, which contains a pass-through to the interiors of cabinets in the bathroom to the south, and a shallow, narrow set of shelves which holds extra toiletries. The light is overhead, in the center of the ceiling. There is a bathmat on the floor, and a wastebasket under the wash basin.

Entry

Actor enters bathroom, turns on light, closes door, removes bathrobe and pajama top, hangs garment on hook on back of door.

(Comment: Location of door, entry, turning on light, and closing door are monitored by a combination of visual and haptic cues; removal of garments is monitored mostly by haptic cues. If the door is closed first, the light is located and turned on by purely haptic cues.)

Urinating and Defecating

The acts are performed while standing at, or sitting on the commode. The appearance and feeling of these acts are familiar enough to all humans (as well as most vertebrates) that they do not require description[4]. In the specific cultural context invoked here, the pajama bottoms need to be lowered before the actor is seated.

(Comment: There are obvious gender distinctions at work in urination; women sit while men stand, as a general rule. Furthermore, after urinating, women wipe while men do not. Defecating shows no such gender distinctions, although there exists a common folk belief that when arranging toilet paper for wiping, women crumple while men fold. As far as I can ascertain, this has never been seriously tested. The release of urine and fecal material is controlled by internal haptic cues, while wiping and flushing are controlled by external haptic cues. There are incidental auditory cues, such as urine splashing and feces dropping, but these do not appear to have significant monitoring implications. Defecation is frequently accompanied or preceded by flatulence. If we look at the wider context, it appears that bathrooms are designed to maintain both acoustical and olfactory isolation from adjacent rooms and their occupants. This explains the common practice of turning on the water in the basin in order to provide a "white noise" to mask the sounds of urination and defecation, and also, the presence of exhaust fans in bathrooms to dispel these personal aromas, or aerosol deodorants to mask them.)

Shaving

Remove pajama, hang on hook

Washing face

Turn on hot water tap, let run until hot.

Hold washcloth under hot water tap, wring out, repeat until hot enough

Rub soap into washcloth.

Scrub face with washcloth.

Rinse out washcloth to remove soapy water.

Rinse soap from face.

(Comment: Each of these subroutines involves repetition of motions until the specified end-state is reached, repetitions corresponding precisely to Chomskyian "recursivity" in sentence-formation. Note that the reaching of the end-state sometimes involves a precise judgment-call.)

Applying shaving cream

Open cabinet door, remove shaving cream can, remove top

Shake shaving cream.

Squirt shaving cream onto first two fingers of right hand.

Spread shaving cream on face.

Starting with base of left sideburn, spread cream down across left cheek to point of chin.

Start from base of right sideburn and repeat.

Pick up gob of cream from point of chin and spread on area under jaw-line down throat to line where whiskers cease to grow.

Spread remaining cream on area above mouth.

Rinse hands to remove remaining shaving cream.

Removing whiskers:

Pick up razor and run under hot water tap to remove chill.

Shave face.

Start with left side-burn, sweep razor down in parallel strokes until the left corner of mouth is reached.

(Comment: This first pass of the razor is also used to determine the remaining sharpness of the blade. If it is too dull, GOTO blade-changing digressive subroutine.[5]

Return to left angle of jaw and begin downward strokes, shaving throat region from left to right, until right handle of jaw is reached.

Starting under right sideburn, sweep razor downward in parallel strokes until right corner of jaw is reached.

Shave around mouth, starting with downward strokes above upper lip, then follow with downward strokes below lower lip, downward strokes on front chin area, and finally with downward strokes on the curved part of the central chin. The upper lip area and the lower lip area are shaved again with upward strokes, and the two regions on either side of the front chin, again with upward strokes.

Rub shaved area with fingertips, in order to determine the adequacy of the shave. Re-shave rough patches.

Rinse razor under hot water tap, return to cabinet.

Check face and throat for cuts, and decide whether medication or bandaging are necessary.

Remoisten washcloth under hot water tap.

Wipe face to remove shaving cream and remaining severed whiskers.

Rinse washcloth again, wring out, and hang on towel rack.

(Comment: If the male face were either a perfect sphere or a perfect cylinder, the actual shaving operation would be less demanding; however, this is emphatically not the case. Thus, the trickiest part of this operation is in shaving around the mouth, where the face contains a number of little dips and protuberances, as well as delicate intersections of skin and mucous membrane. Unsurprisingly, cuts of the skin occur most frequently in this region. This delicate monitoring operation involves keeping the center of the blade doing the actual cutting, to avoid the digging in of corners, and keeping the blade moving at an angle of 30 or 60 degrees to the direction of the razor motion, in order to avoid both the slashing that results from moving the blade directly in line with the razor's path, and the simultaneous digging in of the entire cutting edge of the blade which results from holding the blade at 90 degrees to the razor's path. And, of course, pressure of the blade against the face must be kept within nominal limits, in order to avoid both the cuts which result from too much pressure, and the failures to cut off whiskers which result from too little pressure. The above presumes the use of a safety razor; men who still shave with a straight razor must monitor an additional set of parameters, while men who use electric shavers clearly must adopt a significantly different algorithm. It should also be noted that despite the custom of performing this sequence in front of a mirror, most of it could be performed in total darkness, since haptic monitoring controls every phase of the operation except checking for cuts. To put it another way, the fingertips and the facial surface are the "eyes" that control the operation.)[6]

Cleaning Teeth

Flossing

Remove box of dental floss from cabinet.

Pull out end of strand of floss, then cut it off at

appropriate length.
Wrap ends of floss around middle fingers of each hand, with most of floss in left middle finger.
Starting with upper left third molar, run floss between adjacent teeth and floss lower corner of each adjoining tooth, working from left to right, and from upper to lower jaw. After each half, of each jaw, take up a turn of the floss from left wrapped finger to right, in order to present a fresh length of floss for the following cleaning segment, and minimize the chance of breaking the floss.
Unwrap floss from fingers and drop into waste-basket.
Return floss box to cabinet.

(Comment: My wife correctly points out that my flossing technique leaves much to be desired. Aside from my irrational dislike of dental hygienists with their pettifogging instructions and imperious manner, I rarely have either the time or the inclination to floss "by the book". The price I pay for this intransigence is the wondering frown of the hygienist as she peers into my mouth prior to prophylaxis.)

Brushing of Teeth

Remove toothbrush from brush-holder, wet bristles under cold tap.

Beginning with upper left back molar, and holding toothbrush horizontally with bristles at a 45-degree angle, insert bristles into upper gum line and wiggle, then turn wrist and move brush head downward. Move brush to right and repeat, finishing with upper right back molar. Repeat with lower jaw. Open mouth wider and clean the back surfaces of the teeth in the order given above, with the brush held in a vertical position.

Return brush to holder.
Fill plastic cup with water, rinse mouth.
Open cabinet door, remove tooth powder can, remove cap from can, pour tooth powder from can into palm of left hand, close cabinet door.
Remove toothbrush from holder, turn on cold tap, remoisten brush under water stream, and dip in tooth powder.
Starting with upper back molar, brush fronts of teeth with vertical movements of toothbrush held in positions specified in previous operation.
Rinse toothbrush under cold water stream, tap handle of toothbrush on side of basin to remove water and residual tooth powder. Repeat two or more times, until brush looks clean.
Return brush to holder.
Refill water cup, rinse mouth two or three times, until water discharged from mouth appears to be clear.
Replace cap on tooth powder can, open cabinet door, return can to shelf, close cabinet door.

(Comment: The repetitive moves in this sequence are not exact repetitions, in that they take place at adjacent locations in the mouth, and are modified in response to differing local conditions [shape of teeth, local shape of oral cavity, and angle of access]. In fact, they bear a formal resemblance the repeating segments of organisms discussed by Bateson, which he used to demonstrate that this sort of configuration was diagnostic of a life-form {Bateson, 1979, }. You will note that, despite the specification of individual acts, locations, and artifacts, I might have chosen to describe each unit in much greater detail. In fact, there appears to be no "natural" cutting point which separates the essential from the unessential detail. To a certain extent, this may be an artifact of trying to recode what are essentially nonverbal algorithms into verbal descriptions. The hands, in carrying out these algorithms, have all the information they need. In addition, the description fails to include the full sweep of the bodily ballet, in that it does not describe what both hands are doing during the same stretch of time, or what the trunk, face, and feet are doing during the hand operations.)

Showering the Body

Remove pajamas bottoms and hang on hook
Remove wrist watch, place on shelf in pass-through.
Open shower enclosure door on tub, step into tub, close door.
Activating water and adjusting water temperature

> Turn on hot tap and let run until hot.
> Turn on cold tap until water emerging from spigot in the comfort range.
> Pull up on valve control on spigot, which diverts water from spigot to shower head.
> Shiver or sweat while readjusting taps to restore water to comfort range.

(Comment: The adjusting of the temperature of the water flow can be exacting, and even frustrating, depending on whether or not someone elsewhere in the building turns on hot or cold water during the shower, which can precipitate unexpected and rapid changes in water temperature. Changes like these may be anticipated to a certain extent by listening for the sound of water running in the pipes before stepping into the shower, an instance of acoustical monitoring used to control haptic adjustments.)

> Turn body around to expose all surfaces to water flow, paying special attention to groin (front and back) and armpits.

Pick up soap from soap dish

(Comment: Edward Hall reminds us that one of our most distinctive features as humans is that we create elaborate anticipations of actions, or "adumbrations" (Hall, 1964: 154-163). In the instant case, if one does not check the state of the soap before stepping into the shower, one discovers that only a tiny, slippery sliver of soap remains, totally inadequate to the task at hand. If one has discovered this prior to entry, obtained a new bar of soap, unwrapped it, and placed it in the soap dish, one may choose to modify the shower procedure by "marrying the soap"; that is, uniting the old sliver with the new bar. Some soap manufacturers thoughtfully provide convenient concavities in their bars to facilitate this delicate operation, while others fiendishly mold their products into curvilinear surfaces which make this operation impossible. In my house, I am known as the "soap chaplain" because of the masterful manner in which I carry out this operation. This is only one of my many titles.)

Rub soap on all surfaces of body, starting with left arm and arm pit, followed by right arm, front of torso from chin to genitals, back of torso from neck to buttocks and anal fissure, right leg from groin to toes, left leg, neck, and ears.
Rinse all body surfaces and crevices, following order given in previous step.
Push down on spigot valve control to return water flow to spigot, and then turn off both taps.
Open shower door.
Step out of shower.
Remove towel from rack.
Towel body dry, starting with face and head, and working one's way south to toes.
Re-hang towel on rack.

(Comments: Among urban middle-class Americans, the showering algorithm, although nominally intended for cleansing the surface of the body, would appear to have little or nothing to do with cleansing. UMCAs are rarely dirty in the physical sense, except when they clean their garages or attics, or work on messy objects such as ovens or the engines of motor vehicles. Showers are usually taken once a day and more frequently if the showerer engages in regular physical exercise, or on the occasion of an anticipated sexual encounter. In my view, the primary function of the shower is the restoration of gumption to the showerer. In simpler terms, showers are fun. The fun arises from the pleasurable haptic sensations which arise from the flow of the water over the surface of the body. Two recent TV commercials bear this out.[6] The first shows a man dragging his semi-anesthetized body into the shower, unwrapping a bar of the sponsor's soap, inhaling its rare essence, engaging in a shower which provides rapture just this side of orgasm, and emerging from the shower with a twinkle in his eye and a spring in his step, ready to fight dragons (small ones, anyway). The second, which carries the hedonism theme even further, shows a young heterosexual couple engaging in "innocent" horseplay in the nude, and even including small children in the merriment. We are invited to believe that a little incest is nothing more than a spicing of the joys of the shower. And even if we decide to be culturally relative about the sexual abuse of children, we are still expected to acknowledge that erotic frolicking is implicit in the enjoyment of the haptics of the experience. This raises the complex issue of the relationship between haptics and eroticism, an issue which is too important to ignore, but too digressive to be dealt with in this essay.)

Final Operations

Removing steam from surface of mirror

Inspect mirror for obscuring moisture.

If moisture found, remove dry washcloth from towel rack.

Wipe mirror surface until it is free of moisture.

Refold washcloth and re-hang on rack.

Applying deodorant

Open cabinet door, remove deodorant container with right hand.

Unscrew cap from deodorant container.

Apply deodorant to left armpit with deodorant container held in right hand, and to right armpit with left hand.

Replace cap on deodorant container.

Open cabinet door and return deodorant container to shelf.

Close cabinet door.

(Comment: UMCAs spend millions of dollars a year on olfactory "niceness", using products such as deodorants, deodorant soaps, mouth washes, breath sprays, douches, groin sprays, and foot and shoe deodorizers. It would seem that olfactory anxieties are among our most treasured personal stresses. To a certain extent, this may be a consequence of our common UMCA language. The statement, "It smells!" does not evoke positive olfactory experience or evaluation, while its rowdy, lower-class cousin, "It stinks!", evokes even more intense olfactory negativity.)

Combing hair

Open cabinet door, remove comb with right hand.

Turn on cold tap.

Wet comb under tap, then run through hair, starting on right side of head, from top of head forward to hair line on forehead. Repeat operation, moving across front of head from left to right. Repeat entire sequence, starting from top of head backward to hair line on nape of neck.

Turn off cold tap.
Starting with remembered location of part on right side of head, use comb to sweep hair to right of part, then repeat, sweeping hair to left of part across center line of head (front-to-back). Comb to both sides of head.
Starting with top of head, sweep hair downward on back of head to rear hair line.[7]
Return comb to cabinet and close door.

Final Cadence

Don pajamas.
Open door.
Turn out light.
Exit bathroom.

DISCUSSION

There is an inevitable transparency to the foregoing description, in that most of its readers are well-bathroomed, and about half of them execute similar routines on a daily basis. The sense of the exotic, a central feature of traditional ethnographic description, is conspicuous by its absence.

I have referred previously to the banality of the algorithms described above. To a certain extent, this is a consequence of the familiarity which we have with these daily operations, and the fact that we execute them so easily that we can allow our attention to be focused on the subjective flow of material going on in our minds, with only occasional attention to the progress of the algorithms being efficiently executed by our clever, capable hands[8]. Another factor in this banality is that these sequences are non-verbal, both in their initial acquisition and their daily repetitions, and that their monitoring is, for the most part, non-verbal.[9]

I should like to continue this discussion by considering the monitoring operation in greater detail, treating the various sensory channels in sequence.

I believe that we generally assume that the visual channel is the most important one for completing these sequences. We usually insist that bathrooms be well-illuminated, and that the mirror above the basin kept free of moisture during the post-shower phases of the operation. And yet, the fact that blind individuals are able to carry out these operations unassisted, for the most part, should go to persuade us that the visual channel is somewhat less salient than usually imagined. Visual monitoring is convenient for entering and leaving the tub, and monitoring the process of hair-combing. It is necessary only for checking for shaving nicks (the use of electric razors making even this one essential function unnecessary). It is possible for a normally-sighted individual to get through the bathroom operation entirely without visual input, as I discovered once when there was a power failure, and there were neither candles nor flashlights in the house. As may be imagined, my execution of these algorithms was both slower and clumsier than it would have been under normal conditions of illumination; however, the point is that it was possible to carry it out successfully.

The acoustical channel is employed even less than the visual; it is used to monitor the force of water-flow both in basin and shower, and as previously noted, may be employed to determine whether water is running elsewhere in the building. Also previously noted was the use of running water to provide a "white noise" barrier to mask the more intimate sounds of bodily activities which are not considered appropriate for acoustical reception by others, even though these others are family members.[10]

The olfactory channel is even less salient. The use of exhaust fans and deodorants has been referred to earlier, as means of concealing corporeal aromas from the perception of others. For some participants, the aromas of soaps, tooth cleansers, and deodorants provide aesthetically pleasing sensations, which presumably enrich the experiences, although not necessary to successful execution. Some of us are sufficiently depraved that we actually enjoy the smell of bodily aromas, but only in the privacy of our own bathrooms, of course.

The gustatory channel appears to function much as does the olfactory channel. Children often appear to enjoy the taste of soap and tooth paste.[11] I recall that, as a child, I was keenly aware of the flavors of such non-food items as medicines, glues, and metal faucets. Even now, an occasional belt of Nyquil goes down "mighty smooth" whether I have a cold or not.[12]

Central to the entire argument is the point that in the operations under consideration here, the haptic sense is of major importance, far outweighing the other sensory channels. Also, among the various haptic inputs, those arising from the hands and fingers are most significant. These control not only the objects held in the hands, but also perceive the actual movements of these objects by the sensations transferred through them to the hands. Especially in the shaving operation, where the visual inputs provide little useful information about how close the whiskers are being cut, the haptic inputs reign supreme. Similarly, in the shower, information about which parts of the body are being scrubbed, and about the adequacy of the coverage, is conveyed by haptic information which arrives simultaneously from the concerned body parts and the hands doing the actual scrubbing. The success of drying body surfaces is determined once again by haptic inputs from the skin.

The adequacy of deodorant application to the armpits is similarly monitored. There is virtually no difference in appearance between a brushed and an un-brushed tooth, claims of toothpaste manufacturers to the contrary notwithstanding.

Instances could be multiplied; however, enough have been supplied to support, at least tentatively, the claims of haptic predominance.

This discussion advances no pretensions to completeness. An obvious omission has been the role of haptic inputs and outputs in correcting misfiring algorithms. Whether is it a dropped bar of soap, a misplaced razor on a cabinet shelf, or an empty toilet roll spindle, the hands need to spring into action with the remedy. Frowning at the miscreant object, or even denouncing it, won't help even a little bit. Hand operations do not inevitably remedy the situation; a bar of soap flung against the wall might relieve the annoyance temporarily, but will just make more cleanups in the end.[13] The patient application of remedial manual algorithms is the only really effective way to deal with such situations.

Another dimension of the argument hitherto neglected is that of actual allocation in time of the execution of the algorithms. A videotape of this operation would reveal that there are major tempo changes that take place during execution, from the *adagio* of movements of the razor, to the brisk *vivace* of toothbrush movements. There are also instances of *ritardando* and *accelerando*, as well as *fermata* that take place before decisive events, such as stepping into the shower, or awaiting the occurrence of the first fecal discharge. Again, this belaboring of the obvious suggests that the tempos and rhythms of every-day life provide the major source of musical expressions within every culture, a point made by

Lomax more than thirty years ago (1970.)

CONCLUSION

This discussion has focused on the package of algorithms specifically located within a particular site, the UMCA bathroom. Future plans include similar descriptions in other locations in the UMCA house: kitchen, workshop, laundry, and garage being obvious choices. Also, this initial description was selected so to include only one-person algorithms; further efforts will include settings within which more than one person regularly interact and, with any luck, cooperate. This may lead to a finer-grained type of description in which not only individual trajectories may be plotted, but also, the sequential use of common space by multiple partners, including body-movement paths and hand-paths, which require a more subtle sharing of space.

The approach may make possible novel comparisons among households at different socio-economic levels, and from different regional and ethnic backgrounds.

Hopefully, this approach may prove of some use to archaeologists, since it has the potential of situating artifacts not only within their behavioral settings, but also, within the algorithmic sequences in which they are employed.

The addition of a sound track to these descriptions may also be helpful to linguists, in that the verbal track may be seen in a richer behavioral setting, with simultaneous staves for the inputs and outputs of the various sensory channels, as well as the kinetic counterpoint to the flow of conversation (Birdwhistell was one of the pioneers in this sort of endeavor [1970].)

And finally, there is a potential for cultural description

that may work in virtually any cultural setting in the world. I believe that any society that has achieved a minimal level of stability of expectation and predictability may be fruitfully viewed as an interconnected bundle of periodic algorithms (hourly, daily, monthly, annually, etc.) which can be described using the common language based on the our common possession of human bodies and common potentials for interpersonal and environmental transactions. And while it is obvious that only a small percentage of the earth's population have regular access to urban middle-class bathrooms, it is simultaneously true that all individuals must cope with acts such a urination and defecation, washing the body partially or totally, shaving or depilating, and arranging hair in culturally specific coiffures. The dispersal of these acts to multiple locations might make the task of description somewhat more complicated, but certainly not impossible. Whether or not this is a valuable procedure is another matter, one that must be critically evaluated by independent judgment.

* * * * * * *

ENDNOTES

1. None of this is particularly original with me; only the assemblage.

2. An important distinction, in dealing with the complex sense of touch, is the contrast between external, medial, and internal Haptics, corresponding to perceptions which takes place at or near the surface of the body, those which arise from receptors within the muscles and joints, and those which arise from within the alimentary canal and other internal organ systems and spaces. This is not a complete map

of haptic sensations, since it ignores the specialized sensations arising from the middle ear, having to do with movement and balance of the body. This will be developed in another place.

3. We need to consider the historical context within which Harris was writing; in the 1960s the quantitative-behaviorist paradigm was still dominant and without serious challengers. And of course, Harris, in his more influential works (1968, 1979), became the leading spokesman for the Cultural Materialist perspective, which continues to owe fealty to quantitative behaviorism.

4. UMCAs learn at an early age that when entering a strange environment, it is of highest priority to locate the rest rooms. On the other hand, the purely unique aspect of these acts for humans is that we are required to anticipate them (sometimes far in advance of the need's becoming pressing), and to be aware of culturally sanctioned locations where they may take place. This may not be much of a problem for a forager in a tropical rain forest, but it can provide a problem of crucial importance for an individual wandering in a large urban area. And of course, the older one becomes, the higher the urgency.

5. This subroutine is as follows:

Open cabinet and remove case of blades.

Unscrew stem of razor to create access to old blade.

Remove old blade, slide into back compartment

of case.

Slide new blade out of case, place in open top of razor.

Screw handle of razor to close top over new blade.

Return blade case to cabinet.

6. An obvious gender bias exists here, in that many women put on makeup as part of their bathroom algorithms, while men shave. Both involve the face; however, the application of makeup obviously involves a much greater degree of visual monitoring and relatively little haptic monitoring, precisely the reverse of the male shaving. In the interests of fairness, not to mention political correctness, I probably should have written, "Most women do not shave, and most men do not apply makeup." Ten years from now, who knows?

7. There is something outrageous about the suggestion that there might be any shred of ethnographic reality to be found in the profit-driven fantasies of TV commercials. And yet, the agencies which inflict these costly, technically astonishing productions on the viewing public are compelled by competitive pressures to please their sponsors by increasing product sales, and are thus bound within the parameters of the values, tastes, and worldviews of urban, middle-class Americans.

8. The alert reader will note that I have omitted hair-washing from the daily routine, which is to some extent a function of relative age. It is my

impression that the average UMCA teenager washes her/his hair at half-hour intervals. Cleanliness would not appear to be the issue here. At the advanced age of 64, I wash my hair every six months or so, whether it needs it or not. Also, the hair configuration resulting from the execution of this algorithm, along with the appropriately style of haircut, is yet another age marker, having been popularized by Harry Truman.

9. I generally get my best ideas concerning forthcoming lectures during the execution of these algorithms (also the worst.)

10. Bateson's illuminating discussion of the unconscious and its contents (Bateson, 1972) shows more resonance with this discussion than do the better-known formulations of Freud, Chomsky, and Levi-Strauss. Bateson appears to understand that "logic" (algorithmic phenomena) is not confined to the verbal level of awareness, as shown by his repeated quotation from Pascal to the effect that "the heart has its reasons, which reason itself knows not."

11. This suggests that Goffman's well-known distinction between "on stage" and "back stage" behavior could use some additional fine-tuning (Goffman, 1965)

12. Toothpaste manufacturers certainly believe this to be the case, given the prominence of claims of "tasting good" in ads for children's tooth paste. Similar claims are advanced for mouth washes, indicating that such gustatory enjoyment is not limited to children.

13. It is even better with diet ginger-ale and ice.

14. Of course, if the flinger realizes that someone else will feel constrained to do the cleanup, then there is an added bonus of revenge, if the "someone else" is in disfavor with the flinger. Most commonly among UMCAs, husbands do the flinging while wives do the cleaning. In households of a nontraditional makeup, one might suspect that the negotiation of these roles may be of major significance to the stability of the association.

Chapter 4: Kitchen Algorithms

This chapter continues the general format and procedure of the previous "Bathroom Algorithms" discussion, organized around algorithms and their settings. The major difference is that the activities in the kitchen are considerably more complex than those of the bathroom, and will therefore require a more extensive treatment. The use of the different rooms of the house as foci for chapters is a novel one, as least as far as I know, for ethnographic descriptions. {I notice that my writing block, of some forty years standing, is completely gone. I credit Piers Anthony with this change; his discussion was incredibly helpful.} Given the conceptual framework of this project, the "house" plan makes good sense; since algorithms are at the heart of the project, organizing them in terms of their customary places of occurrence seems to be the way to proceed. (See Chapter 1 for the laying out of this conceptual scheme.) This essay will connect with other portions of the overall project: *Voyaging the Alimentary Canal* will pick up the theme of food processing from the lips on down; the use of sinks and wash basins will connect with *Bathroom Algorithms*, The technology of hand tools and algorithms will connect with *Workshop Algorithms,* etc.

My concern here is that vast repertory of algorithms that constitute the interface between the human needs for aliment and their satisfaction. In the urban, middle-class culture of the contemporary U. S., these algorithms reside, for the most part, in the kitchen, occasionally leaking out into the dining room, living room, family room, and bedrooms for actual food consumption. Food preps, however, are almost exclusively confined to the kitchen area.

Settings

In describing the algorithms associated with the preparation and serving of food, as well as the cleanup which follows, I need to pay some systematic and detailed attention to the settings in which these things happen.

Kitchens, in most urban areas of the world, are complicated places, compared to bathrooms. Given the obsession of USians with technology, their contemporary kitchens are probably among the most complicated on earth. Many if not most of the repetitive hand motions common to most food-producing activities can now be carried out with electrical machinery. And if you believe the commercials on the Shopping Networks, and the many overheated infomercials elsewhere on the Cable, there continues to be an almost unlimited appetite for even more culinary gadgetry. Now, I grant the focused ethnocentrism of this discussion. Food has been prepared in an astounding variety of cultural settings, from the camp fires of hunting bands to the vast kitchens of monarchs, or the highly professionalized, intense kitchens of up-scale, trendy restaurants in New York or San Francisco; while acknowledging this, I have no plan for trying to deal with this range of variation.

Here I am dealing specifically with the home kitchen. The professional kitchens differ not only in scale but also in intensity, involving large numbers of people, organized into complicated patterns of social interaction. The home kitchen by contrast, assumes only a single cook, (although we know that occasionally two or more people cooperate in the preparation of a meal). In communitarian societies, such as the Hutterites, we find a larger cooking crew which operates more like an expanded one-person kitchen than a scaled-down professional kitchen. I will proceed by first discussing the physical circumstances and conditions of the kitchen, followed by the clean-up operations which are necessary to keep the kitchen in good working order. I will conclude with a discussion of the symbolism of food preparation and service, and a concluding note on the historical context of food preparation and consumption in the United States.

Material Storage

The materials we deal with in the kitchen are food stuffs, utensils, and devices. Kitchens have long functioned as storage areas for food stuffs. We can distinguish between proximal storage, which includes materials that will be used frequently in the preparation of meals, and distal storage, or long term storage, for materials that are either used infrequently, or stored in a large quantity and used to replenish proximal items when the supply is running out. A century and a half ago, root cellars and pantries were common sites for distal storage. Over the past century, the development of food technology, particularly refrigerators and freezers, has made it possible to store things over long periods of time with less deterioration of the foods. In today's urban middle-class kitchen, we find a great deal of storage space in the form of numerous cupboards and cabinets.

Utensils over the same period of time have proliferated in amazing ways. They have become more numerous and more specialized. Our great-grandmothers would have been amazed at the arrays of garlic presses, wire whisks, mandolins, and nutmeg graters. Mechanical devices have also undergone an astonishing radiation, adding both convenience and extra operations to the cook's repertory, but require additional counter space for accessibility and a substantially increased power supply.

Working Space

Actual food preparations take place in front of the body in the region extending from the crotch to just below the sternum. Therefore the various surfaces such as counter tops, table tops, cutting boards and sinks, are all located within this zone for the maximal comfort and convenience of the cook. It is within this domain that the preparation and assembling of food take place.

Temperature Control

Many of the devices found in the modern kitchen are involved in temperature control. Stoves, microwaves, deep fat fryers, and electric devices such as bread machines and rotisseries, are designed to produce controlled levels of high heat, while refrigerators, deep freezers, and ice cream machines similarly produce low temperatures. Many kitchens are equipped with exhaust fans which serve the dual function of cooling the kitchen, and removing smoke.

At the most basic level, the sensation of temperature is a haptic one, since the nerve endings in the skin respond directly to temperature changes in the environment.

Food preparation almost always involves control of temperature variations which go beyond the range of comfort of the skin on the hands, thus shifting the monitoring function from haptic to visual. The professional chef regularly employs extremes of temperature that go beyond those of the amateur cook. His stoves are hotter, and his refrigerators and freezers are usually colder. This is one of the reasons that grease fires are so much commoner in professional kitchens than in home kitchens. High heat is more problematic than extreme cold; there is not much reason to chill something colder than 0 degrees Fahrenheit. High heat, such as required for baking, deep-fat frying or cooking candy, is an inherently dangerous working condition. A tipped container could result in a serious fire, and/or serious burns for the chef. This is why professional chefs use thermometers, not only to avoid disasters, but also, because small differences in the temperature of the hot medium can result in major differences in the texture of the food. Some preparations, such as for french-fries, require two or more successive cookings in oils of different temperature.

Utilities

Kitchens require specialized utilities such as hot and cold water, water drains, and electricity. Like bathrooms, kitchens are plumbed separately into the house's water system. The water supply for the kitchen can also have its own filtering system. One or more sinks will be equipped with hot and cold water and drains, while fancier kitchens will have a water supply running to the refrigerator for the making of cold water and ice, and a separate cold water tap over the stovetop.

In terms of electrical supply, kitchens need to be well lighted, which usually involves ceiling fixtures, as well as spot lighting over some work surfaces. And while the kitchen of a hundred years ago could get by with a couple of wall plugs, the modern kitchen requires multiple electrical outlets to accommodate the wide variety of electrical appliances and devices.

Information Sources

Most cooks require sources for recipes. This usually involves cookbooks, which require their own shelf space. In some contemporary kitchens, the computer has become indispensable, both for calling up recipes out of files on the hard drive, and for accessing the internet as a source of recipes, demonstrations, and other valuable information.

Algorithms

Everything that has proceeded in this essay has been setting the stage of the actual operations by which food is handled and produced in the kitchen. We will handle this under four basic sections: preparations, presentation, channels and monitoring, and clean-up.

Preparations

Handpaths and Footpaths

Unlike computer algorithms, which take place in computer space (covered elsewhere), human algorithms take place in the mundane world, which is three-dimensional, filled with fuzzy categories and clutter. The primary way that we humans deal with this space is by way of customary algorithms, which involve hands and sometimes, feet. We almost never stop to invent novel pathways for these useful parts of the body; instead, we follow familiar algorithmic itineraries: handpaths and footpaths.

In most if not all human cultures, foot paths are the most obviously coded. Maps are the prime example, whether those of the Micronesian navigator, which organize hundreds of miles of open ocean into recognizable segments, or those Trip-ticks which one can get from the Auto Club, which segment a long driving trip into recognizable portions. Large regions tend to be more explicitly coded than do small areas, probably because they are less intuitively obvious (coded haptically) than the small ones.

I can think of no obvious examples of clearly coded hand paths, although the stylized hand movements of Southeast Asian, South Asian, and Middle Eastern dance may represent non-technological segments of hand paths (but, see Alan Lomax on Choreometrics). Musical practice and performance constitutes a huge area for hand and finger paths, and needs to be explored in this framework, since none of the text materials usually used in ethnomusicology courses pay much attention to the actual physical processes involved in the making of music. Time-and Motion studies in the US focused on hand paths in the context of industrial work, with the limited goal of determining the most "efficient" way to accomplish a given set of repetitive tasks. (These eventually fell out of favor, since they failed to take into account other factors concerning worker motivation, such as fatigue, boredom, and manual display.)

In the kitchen, footpaths mark the spaces where the cook moves to carry out the various tasks. Kitchen designers of thirty years ago decided that the critical triangle is marked by the stove, the refrigerator, and the prep surface. The idea is that the smaller the triangle, the more efficient the preparations.

Hand paths involve a number of distinct operations from the location of recipes and the assembling of utensils and food stuffs, to the actual processing of foods and the production of foods to be served. Recipes constitute an unusually pure example of written algorithms. Recipes consist of two parts, a list of ingredients (usually in the order in which they are used), and the steps to follow for the preparation. Recipes are as interesting in what they leave out as in what they present. The recipe writer assumes that the user of the recipe has at their disposal a kitchen such as the one described previously in this essay, and has the basic hand skills necessary for following the recipe.

Experienced cooks will do things other than strictly following printed recipes. Sometimes they make minor alterations in printed recipes, such as substituting lime zest for lemon zest. Sometimes, cooks will create novel dishes either under the pressure of the shortened time frame for getting the meal on the table, or at other times from the sheer desire to innovate and create something new. Either process might produce results which range from culinary disasters to the triumphant creation of a major new dish.

Presentations

Sensory Channels and Monitoring the Algorithms

Much of the skill of the cook depends on her (his) ability to monitor the stage-wise progression of the processes of preparation and cooking. This monitoring involves the various sensory channels; visual (colors, surfaces, quantities), auditory (coming to a boil, the onset and progress of sizzling, the sound of the "thump" of a properly baked loaf), olfactory (initial state of ingredients, smell of mixtures at various stages, changes during cooking of sauces and gravies, approaches to the stage of doneness), gustatory (tasting at all stages of preps) and haptic (weights, temperatures, and textures of utensils and ingredients, resistance to spoon while mixing, feel of dough while kneading, resistance to spoon while stirring, completion of pan-scraping, completion of the cutting of shortening into flour, perception of both constant and changing surfaces).

This kind of monitoring process is remarkably complex, involving as it does all of the external sensory channels. Of course, the more complicated the recipe, the more demanding the monitoring. And if we add to the performance the consideration that an professional cook is usually running more than one assembly algorithm (possibly as many as six at a time), and then the management of the various algorithms, all within a fairly strictly defined time frame, becomes a fair demonstration of the limits of human ability to carry out such complex operations successfully. After all, the meal usually arrives at the table in time and in good order, with the hot foods hot and the cold foods cold.

This might be compared with the task of the symphony conductor, who must monitor and control many lines of individual performances, in order to achieve a satisfactory realization of the composer's intent. However, in terms of the sensory demands, the conductor has an easier task, since the monitoring is primarily done in the auditory channel, secondarily in the visual channel, but without involving the other channels in any significant way. It doesn't matter a particle what a musician smells like, so long as he (she) produces the right sounds at the right moments.

It has been asserted air traffic controllers, while monitoring many planes arriving and departing at major air fields, are engaged in the most complex multitasking which humans are capable of performing. To this assertion, I would add two observations:

1) It must be admitted that the air traffic controllers are in vastly more stressful situations than the cook. The worst that could happen if the cook "drops the ball" would be a disappointing meal and embarrassment for the cook (and possibly, firing). A similar failure of the air traffic controller could cause a disaster of monumental proportions. The amount of stress in a given situation would undoubtedly affect the level of performance, but not necessarily the complexity of the tasks.
2) In the sense of this argument, the tasking of the air traffic controller is simpler than that of the cook, in that the air traffic controller needs to monitor closely only the visual and acoustical channels, the haptic channel only trivially (the control of the buttons and switches on the control panel), and the gustatory and olfactory channels not at all.

Various tools are employed in the process of executing the steps described in this chapter. We have not included a section on the development of tools, though this has been a long standing subject of speculation among historians and anthropologists. Viewed from the standpoint of haptic theory, tools are for the most part, extensions and improvements on parts of the human body. The screwdriver and tools which perform scraping and cutting functions substitute and improve on fingernails and teeth. (Many a houses wife knows that her right thumbnail is a very useful cleaning tool.) The hammer improves on the fist. Vices, pliers and grippers of various sorts substitute for the grip between the thumb and fingers. One glaring exception to this is the wheel. The inventor was clearly thinking outside the box or the body. The fact that the wheel does not have a counterpart in the human body is what makes this particular invention a dazzling display of creativity. The computer is loosely based on the human brain, and the tasks it normally performs.

Chapter 5: Voyaging the Alimentary Canal (A Gastro-Intestinal Tract)

(Why these labels? "Alimentary" implies that food processing is the only function of this system, while "Gastro-Intestinal" merely names two principal components of the passage, the stomach and the intestines. Why not, equally defensibly, call it the "Bucco-Anal" tract, using the starting and ending points as labels? Obviously, the answer is because of the polarized symbolisms of mouth and anus, which I endeavor to come to terms with in another essay. Another option based on function: the "Respiratory-Alimentary" tract.)

This differs from the treatment one might find in a standard medical text in that it is less technical (and less informed), and that it proceeds from a novel viewpoint. From the viewpoint of the individual whose internal sensations are under discussion, these activities and events are both perceived and monitored, for the most part, by aspects of the senses of touch. The interior of the mouth and the upper portion of the throat can be seen, but from there on down, the sense of sight has nothing to contribute. Hearing does play a minor role in providing information concerning events which take place lower in the tract; however, perceptions of pain, pressure, and temperature are more important. Much has been studied and written about the senses of taste and smell, which I will not deal with to any great extent, except to show how these are interrelated with the haptic sensations,

The Mouth: Grand Central Station

When I was about eight years old, I listened regularly to a radio program called *Grand Central Station*, a weekly series of short stories loosely organized around the premise that Grand Central Station, in New York City, was the "cross-road of a thousand busy lives." As a basis for a series, it was pretty lame; but as a metaphor for the human mouth, it seems like a useful image. And, if I were to try to update this metaphor, I would probably go with O'Hare or LAX airports, although neither have quite the right ring to them.

The mouth is the locus of a remarkable array of activities, some of which may take place simultaneously. Much of this complexity arises from the fact that the mouth is the intersection of two systems, the gastric system (intake and swallowing of liquids and solids) and the respiratory system (the delivery of air to the lungs and expulsion of exhalant to the outside, but including phonation of various sorts, such as talking, singing, shrieking, laughing, humming, etc.) It is therefore unsurprising that occasionally materials come to be misdirected (the swallowing of air, the inhaling of liquids or solids into the trachea).

The design problem is that these two systems actually cross in the throat, the respiratory system starting in the nose and descending into the throat, where it crosses from back to front to reach the trachea, and the gastric system starting in the mouth and descending into the throat and going from front to rear to reach the esophagus, Traffic control is then especially tricky when both systems function simultaneously, and the case when we eat and talk at the some time, or even eat and breathe.

I had originally started with a list of events taking place exclusively or partially located in the mouth. This list included feeding, drinking, breathing, signaling, vomiting, licking, sucking, kissing, talking, internal cleaning, singing, snuffling, spitting, sneezing, coughing, sighing, belching, and choking. And although this list of oral functions does provide a starting platform for this discussion, it clearly has its weaknesses. Traditional taxonomies are built on the assumption that the labeled categories are internally homogeneous and externally sharply bounded, which is clearly not the case in considering the mouth; many of these functions go on simultaneously, and involve common mouth parts. In addition, some activities are spread through not only the upper portion of the GI tract, but also involve the trachea-lungs segment and\or the esophagus\stomach segment. Of necessity, I am employing folk taxa from American English; there is no other set of terms available that I know of, and besides, I want to communicate with readers, with whom I presumably share these terms.

Feeding: Intake of Solids and Liquids; chewing, mixing, swallowing

The mouth is the original blender and food processor. Long before we had such mechanical devices to take the work out of food preparation, our mouths were capable of reducing all manner of food stuffs to the consistency of baby food, which is the usual consistency necessary for normal swallowing.

What we usually identify as the sense of taste is quite complex; in addition to the four chemical senses located on different portions of the tongue, there is a simultaneous perception of olfactory signals from the nose, as well as the haptic sensations of temperature, texture, and moisture. Traditional cookbooks paid scant attention to the haptics of taste, on the other hand, the sense of touch provides a number of different qualities in the food.

Temperature, a key variable, spans the range from cold to burning hot, with the additional complication that foods with a component of capsaicin, found in the various peppers, creates a perception of heat without any rise in temperature in the inside of the mouth. Control of temperature while eating is a major factor in the aesthetics of dining. We see this in courses that alternate between cold, hot, and room temperature, but also in the actual eating process where the addition of hot beverages such as coffee will warm the temperature of the mouth contents, while the use of chilled beverages or solids will correspondingly cool the contents.

The perception of liquids or moist food generally, can be originally classified as watery or oily; however, the process of mixing in the mouth tends to create emulsions, blends of oil and water. These mixtures are not only a major vehicle of flavors, but serve the vital function of lubrication, both for moving food around in the mouth, but more importantly in making possible the act of normal swallowing.

Foods vary dramatically in their texture. From the dry crunchiness of rice cakes to the silky smoothness of Hollandaise sauce, with varying side textures such as the fibery texture of corned beef and the crisp wetness of watermelon. Textures can change dramatically during the chewing process, with the solids being crushed into smaller and smaller particles and finally reduced to a moist paste. There are a few foods, such as carrots and coconut, which sullenly refuse to be reduced to a smooth paste, and must be swallowed, a mixture of tiny hard particles, which can cause serious problems while being swallowed. Another dimension of texture has to do with the resistance of the food to the chewing process. Some foods chew very easily and are ready to swallow after relatively short processing period, while other foods such as tough meats might require extensive chewing, and may even be swallowed before being reduced to a smooth paste. Another textural sensation having to do with liquids rather than solids is the perception of effervescence, in which a chilled carbonated beverage warms immediately upon striking the tongue and releases its gas contents, producing that "sparkling" sensation.

Of the various food groups, the fats play a vital role not only in flavor (in that they carry the fat-soluble flavorings) but also in their role as lubricants. During normal swallowing, the fat content of the food will form a film in the inside of the mouth, down to the esophagus. Food that is low in fat may cause problems in swallowing, which is one reason why some older people will tend to eat foods with higher fat and oil content, so that they can swallow them more easily.

The process of swallowing, which most of us take for granted, actually involves the simultaneous closing of the larynx, the relaxing of the glottis, and the compression of the mouth contents by raising the tongue to the top of the mouth. The timing of these events is kind of tricky; closing of the larynx too late can result in food being squirted into the upper part of the trachea, while the relaxing of the glottis prematurely can result in air being swallowed with the food. There is always some air present in the mouth while swallowing, however too much air can result in two different outcomes; an airlock can form at the base of the esophagus, or large amounts of air in the stomach which need to be belched out.

Another group of mouth functions has to do with internal cleaning. After swallowing, there are frequently small bits of one kind or another floating around in the mouth; the tongue hunts these down and sends them to the rear to be swallowed. The use of a toothbrush and dental floss are designed to make the cleaning functions more efficient and complete. Another aspect of the cleaning functions takes place when something really unpalatable is taken into the mouth and one has the choice of swallowing or spitting it out.

Not only do we take things into the mouth and swallow them, but occasionally we discharge them as well. Vomiting, spitting, and belching are all instances. The mouth, with its huge array of sensory inputs, performs the vital function of monitoring whatever comes in. Things which are determined at first taste to be unacceptable are spat out. Some internal fluids are given the same treatment: phlegm from the trachea, and mucus from the nose, both turn up regularly in the mouth, either to be swallowed or spat. In point of fact, the process of masticating food and preparing it to swallow, often include not only saliva, but also phlegm and mucus. These liquids differ in viscosity, and might interfere with the swallowing process. Taking pills is frequently done when phlegm is coating the upper part of the throat down to the glottis, with the result that pills can stick in various places, and not go down normally. This is why people commonly take pills with a glass of cold water, since hot water would dissolve the pills in the mouth. For successful pill-taking, one should always take a swallow of water before swallowing the pills, since the water will provide an aqueous layer over the coating of phlegm in the throat, thus facilitating the normal swallowing.

Breathing: Inhaling and Exhaling

Given the complex nature of events that take place within the mouth, and given the real possibility that the process can misfire in various ways, it is hard to understand how the upper Gastro-Intestinal (G.I.) tract could have evolved as it did. As far as we know from the evolutionary record, the different parts of the G.I. tract evolved at different times. The primitive digestive tract goes back to ancient water living creatures that were little more than cylinders made up of double layers of single cells, the inside of which eventually evolved into the gastric tract. As our ancestors became larger and more complex, the gastric tract became more highly specialized for processing food, and developed more complex organs such as the liver, whose secretions aided in the digestive process, as well as providing other vital functions. It wasn't until our ancestors emerged from the water that the respiratory function, which previously consisted of the mouth taking in water and passing it down over the gill bars and past the gills, took an entirely different direction, with the primitive swim bladder being redefined as lungs for extracting oxygen from the air as opposed to the water. This involved major functional changes as the gastric tract became the gastro-respiratory tract. Unlike the previous arrangement which extracted oxygen from the water, it was now necessary to extract oxygen from the air and exhale carbon dioxide into the air, which involved the regular alternation of inhaling and exhaling, from a unidirectional flow of water, to a bidirectional flow of gases.

Normal respiration varies in its tempo from rapid panting during vigorous exercise to slow sustained breathing during sleep. Even more extreme states of respiration are experienced when under a life threatening attack, or when in a deep coma or meditative state. Episodic within normal breathing are events such as sneezing (to clear the nasal passages), and coughing (which clears the upper trachea).

Phonation: (Talking, Singing, Sighing, Grunting, Humming)

As humans, we have added another layer of functions to the respiration and nutritional functions discussed above. And although it is true that a variety of non-human animals produce a tremendous variety of vocalizations and calls, from the trumpeting of elephants to the tiny squeaks of mice and bats, we humans have added the complex coding of speech and language to the primitive calls systems used by nonhuman animals.

What this means is that the vital six inches from the glottis to the mouth, in addition to feeding and breathing, is now required to produce long strings of sounds that make up utterances. We frequently talk while we are eating and breathing, which makes the problem of traffic control in the throat even more complicated. Singing, which involves longer and sustained stretches of phonation, places even greater demands on the breathing mechanism in that it is necessary to inhale large amounts of air, and carefully release it over a longer stretch of time than is found in normal speech.

If we look at this in terms of evolution, it is apparent that the parts of the speech tract evolved over millions of years before our ancestors employed them for verbal communication. And because of this peculiar evolutionary history, various parts of this tract alternately grew and shrank, and were continuously redefined in terms of their biological function. During the last 5 million years, while our ancestors were becoming differentiated from the Great Apes, our brains were getting larger and the top of the skull was increasing in size, while the lower part of the facial skeleton was getting smaller. This means that in the speech tract, things that were once very large, like the tongue, the mandibles, and the hard and soft palates, were shrinking in size. However, the nerve endings which service these regions were getting crowded more closely together, without losing any of their sensitivity.

If we look at the phonetic capabilities of the chimpanzees, we see that they can produce most of the human vowel noises, but are sorely lacking in their abilities to produce consonant sounds. On the other hand, we know that human languages employ a tremendous variety of sounds generated by the speech tract, a variety which would be impossible if we were not all provided with basically the same anatomical equipment.

The Throat

Although we have already been talking about functions of the throat, we now want to address the haptic sensations that are associated with this vital region. We know that at the upper end, air comes by way of the nasal passages, where food comes by way of the mouth. Lower in the throat, there are two tubes that serve different functions. The pharynx, which opens into the trachea, which we use for respiration, and the glottis, which opens into the esophagus, which in turn conducts solids and liquids into the stomach. These two tubes have entirely different haptic sensations. The pharynx-trachea stays open most of the time, and indeed the trachea is surrounded by rings of cartilage, which insures that the airway is open at most times. The esophagus on the other hand, is flat and closed, except while swallowing or regurgitating. The haptic consequences of this is that we are continuously aware of air going in and out of the trachea, while we are only aware of the passages through the esophagus from time to time. In addition to normal swallowing, we sometimes are aware that food gets stuck in the esophagus before it passes through the valve into the stomach. This can be a very painful sensation, because it puts pressure on the heart, because it is in the vicinity of the heart. Drinking some liquid is often helpful in flushing out such a clog, but it gets painful because the pressure builds up before the contents are released into the stomach.

The Stomach

The stomach is a large muscular sack, capable of holding several pounds of semi-liquid contents. Part of its function is biochemical, since it produces both hydrochloric acid and enzymes which aid in the digestive process. And while we do not receive haptic messages from particular locations in the walls of the stomach, we do receive haptic messages from the stomach as a whole. When we have been without food for several hours, we are aware of rhythmic contractions of the stomach walls, which we have learned to identify as hunger pangs. While we are eating a meal, we may be aware of the stomach gradually expanding and filling, and by the time the stomach is completely full, we are certainly aware of that "stuffed" sensation. During normal digestion, the pylorus (the valve at the bottom of the stomach) opens from time to time, and allows portions of the contents of the stomach to flow out into the upper portion of the small intestine. The water contained in the swallowed food is, for the most part, absorbed directly by the veins in the wall of the stomach. On occasions when we have swallowed something inedible, this initiates the vomiting sequence, in which the stomach contracts violently, opening the valve at the top, and hurling the contents of the stomach up the esophagus and out the mouth, and sadly sometimes into the nasal passages. Furthermore, on very rare occasions, contents from the upper part of the small intestine, solid, liquid, or gaseous, passes through the pylorus back into the stomach, causing indigestion, and flatulent-smelling belches.

The Small Intestine

For the most part, we do not receive haptic sensations from the intestines. Occasionally, we feel and hear the movement of gasses as bubbles in the semi-liquid intestinal contents, technically known as borborygmus. Ordinarily, the process of absorption of nutrients into the villi, which line the walls of the small intestine, takes place without feedback to the awareness. I have read that on rare occasions when blockages occur in the small intestine, it causes acute sensations of pain. I have noticed occasionally that intestinal gas can concentrate at the top of the loop next to the diaphragm, which is next to the heart, producing coronary-like sensations.

The Colon

While I was growing up during the 1930's, I was a member of a family in which it was taboo to refer to anything that took place in the body between the waist and the knees, the portions to which the Monty Pythons referred to as "the nasty bits". During my lifetime, and particularly during the past thirty years, there has been a discernable relaxation of the verbal taboos referring to this portion of the body, although it has been celebrated in the context of male humor, or "dirty jokes" for generations. Taking advantage of this new lexical liberality, I want to discuss the haptics of the large intestine.

For the most part, we are not aware of the contents of the colon until the pressure begins to build up in the bottom six inches of the colon, also known as the rectum. As humans, we have much keener sensations in this area than do even our close relatives, the apes. When apes experience fullness, they merely relax and expel the contents of their colons. As humans, who live in social as well as physical environments, we are required to constrain our rectal expulsions as to time and place. As a consequence, we need to become aware of precursory sensations prior to the anal discharge, so that we can reach an appropriate location in time. Thus, our rectums have developed perceptual sensitivities to distinguish among various forms of pressure in the rectum, ranging from actual gas through solids of various consistencies, to watery liquid. This is not biologically given knowledge, but rather is a learned, usually rather painfully through the process of rectal socialization. (Margaret Mead's early work was scornfully dismissed by some of her critics as "diaper anthropology"!) As growing children and adults, we cannot afford to make mistakes in these perceptions, since errors in this area can cause extreme social embarrassment and humiliation, as well as being quite messy. Actually, mammals other than humans are capable of exercising some constraint on their bowel discharges. The experimenters who first socialized the chimpanzee Washo found that it was possible to train her to use the potty most of the time. As far as we know, they never managed to induce much of a sense of guilt for occasions when Washo "missed". We know that cats can be trained to use the cat box, and dogs can be trained to wait to be taken outside.

Under normal circumstances, the sensation of fullness is followed by the discharge of rectal contents, with only a minimum of grunting and straining. However, and particularly as one moves into old age, normal elimination becomes problematic, and constipation is a result. Successful old age involves in part developing coping mechanisms for coaxing the feces into the toilet bowl. These mechanisms range from laxatives, suppositories and fingers, to enemas. And like most magical formulae, sometimes they work, and sometimes they don't. Of course, the amount of vegetable roughage in the diet is a major deterrent as to the frequency and severity of this problem. The problems with constipation do not end with discharge, since an occasional offering will be buoyant, giving rise to the phenomenon of the "floater", which sometimes is more difficult to flush.

We have now finished our first tour of the gastro-intestinal tract. We have viewed the scenic wonders, listened to the internal thunder, and sampled the complex haptics of the mouth, throat, stomach, and rectum. The major point that we have made here is that this crucially important area of the anatomy is known to us largely through haptic sensations, and generally processed non-verbally.

My original plan included a discussion of the bladder and genitals, under the heading, "The Anus and Its Rowdy Neighbors". This topic is too important to be avoided, although its placement within the larger framework of these essays is more problematic. Anatomically, it belongs in this chapter. As I develop the extended discussion of the symbolism of the interior of the body, it will be crucial to include genital symbolism, given its importance in virtually all human societies.

Chapter 6: Algorithms VS Heuristics

What does "heuristic" mean? According to Webster's Dictionary, heuristic means, "encouraging a person to learn, discover, understand, or solve problems on his or her own, as by experimenting, evaluating possible answers or solutions, or by trial and error: *a heuristic teaching method*" or "of, pertaining to, or based on experimentation, evaluation, or trial-and-error methods." My father's definition of heuristic, from the glossary, is "Any bundle of strategies designed to produce a desired outcome or result. Unlike the algorithm, the heuristic cannot be represented by the formal limitation set given above. Generally, heuristics are larger patterns of organized behavior, and may include more than one actor, and/or devices such as a random number generator which violate the algorithmic requirements of finiteness or sequentiality. Heuristics may contain one or more algorithms, frequently as options or subroutines."

I find it noteworthy that although the chapters which he completed prior to his death deal extensively with algorithms and haptics, he says almost nothing about heuristics. He did use the following example to illustrate the difference between algorithms and heuristics: "Making a rabbit stew can be reduced to an algorithm, but *catching* the rabbit is a heuristic." This, at least, is true if you hunt the rabbit as opposed to trapping it.

My father, Donald Crim, argued that many activities in human existence are inherently algorithmic in nature. To a degree this is true. One good example is that of people working on an assembly line. They have a set series of steps that are repeated many times during every work shift, and as much as possible, the steps should be performed in exactly the same way every time, with the intention that the results be as close as possible to identical in every instance.

Other times, an activity might be more algorithmic or more heuristic based on the context. Take painting a house as an example. If you are a contractor hired to paint a group of houses in a suburban subdivision, you might develop algorithms to make the work go more efficiently and produce consistent results. However, if the same contractor is painting his own home out in the country, he might use his creativity to come up with more beautiful and aesthetic results, even if it takes a lot longer than painting one house in a suburb. The context then would determine whether an algorithm or a heuristic would be used to produce a desirable result.

Some activities, such as a musical performance, are more naturally heuristic than algorithmic in nature. Further, activities that depend upon feedback from another person or living being are difficult to boil down to a simple algorithm. Giving your lover a massage or your wife an orgasm are examples of this. To do a good job of it, you must adapt on the fly and adjust what you are doing based on continual feedback coming from the person you are touching. It would be almost impossible to reduce the steps in giving someone an orgasm down to an algorithm, and even if it were possible, your efforts probably would not meet with much appreciation.

However it seems worth mentioning that when someone performs the same act over and over again in a business situation, they are more likely to use algorithms rather than heuristics. If a person is a masseur and gives many massages every day, he is more likely to depend on algorithms than if a person is giving a massage to a loved one, in which the feedback from the person being massaged will be a higher priority and guide the amount of pressure being applied to various parts of the person's body. Similarly, a prostitute might depend much more heavily on algorithms to perform fellatio or manually stimulate their customers to orgasm than a woman performing the same service for her husband.

It appears that when people are being paid to accomplish a task, they are more likely to employ algorithms, where when people perform the same task for the purpose of pleasure or for their own personal reasons, they are more likely to use heuristics.

In Chapter 3 "Bathroom Algorithms", my Dad described his algorithm for shaving. He used a straight razor his entire life, decades after electric razors such as the Norelco were invented and available to the general public. He also performed this algorithm exactly the same every day, and at the same time every day, day after day, week after week, and decade after decade. My approach to shaving is more of a heuristic than an algorithm.

I use a disposable razor or an electric razor, but I never decide which to use until after I have examined how long my facial hair has grown, and have decided what parts of my face I am going to shave, which might vary from day to day, if I bother to shave at all. If I plan to interact with human society on a particular day, I am much more likely to shave, but it is still not a certainty. I might trim my mustache, but I sometimes shave it off because it bothers me. I usually let it grow, because I think many women like it, as do my pets and my mother. If parts of my facial hair have grown so long that it causes itching and discomfort, I am more likely to shave at least some of my face. However, I might choose to shave only a small portion of it, as little as just one strip. I don't even bother to be symmetrical about it. I might shave after showering, which makes the task easier, or I might wet my face down with water if I did not shower. Other times, I shave just using some shaving cream, or just shave dry (which is easier with a sharp razor.) How I shave, whether I shave, how much I shave, when I shave and what facial areas I shave vary on a daily basis. For me, shaving is a heuristic experience, not an algorithmic one.

I believe that whether a person uses an algorithm or a heuristic depends heavily upon the individual and what is comfortable for him. It is not just dependant upon the nature of the task being performed.

My Dad was someone who was comforted by reducing his daily activities to algorithms, where I prefer to approach life in general with heuristic behaviors as opposed to algorithmic ones. One might find it ironic that where he was a Cultural Anthropologist, I am a computer scientist, and therefore am deeply and intimately familiar with the algorithmic nature of computers and the way they execute instructions. Assuming that my father and I both belong to and represent different examples of various human personality archetypes, there are probably some people who are more comfortable approaching the various tasks in their lives using algorithms, where others are more comfortable using a heuristic approach.

It might also be useful to view the use of algorithms as opposed to the use of heuristics on an analog scale, meaning that every individual human being will combine the use of these different approaches in his own unique way. Some people like Dad might tend to rely heavily on the algorithmic approach, others, like me will be inclined to approach every situation in a different way each time it is encountered, and use environmental feedback when tailoring the steps used in the task to accomplish the same goal differently each time. I find it likely that there are other people in the middle of the scale, who use an equal mix of algorithms and heuristics. Again, the context of the situation will often have a bearing upon which approach is chosen by the individual.

Whether algorithms or heuristics are used in creating the steps in a task to accomplish a goal, haptics, or sensory feedback from the sense of touch, are used to execute the steps and frequently effect both the selection of steps and the motivation for the goal. The sense of touch is not the only influence upon human behavior, as instincts coded at the level of DNA also often have a very strong influence.

Regardless of what causes the motivation for a person to display a particular behavior or set a particular goal, haptics are employed to execute algorithms and heuristics to accomplish the desired goal. One does one's best to accommodate motivations caused by human instinct by means of haptic feedback. Haptic feedback often influences the motivations of an individual.

For instance, if a small child who has not yet learned the nature of fire sticks her finger in a flame, the sensory feedback of pain will provide motivation for her to avoid repeating that behavior. However, in most animal life forms, it is also an instinct to fear fire and flames (and smoke for that matter.) If a person is then caught inside a burning house, his motivation to escape is created both my his instinctive fear of fire, as well as his memory of painful sensory feedback experienced by coming into contact with fire in his past.

I conclude that both algorithms and heuristics are employed to accomplish goals, and the motivations to establish goals are based on both instincts and haptics.

Chapter 7: Interpersonal & Intrapersonal Haptics

The Personal Note - Digging Each Other's Act

And so, Pat and I discover that we are audience for each other; in fact, we are not only the best, but usually the only audience for each other, and that we ought to be content with this. My image is of each of us as street musicians, playing to an audience of one, although occasionally and hopefully, one or two other people might stop by and drop a nickel or two into the hat. If we do, eventually, manage to collect a larger audience, that would be wonderful; however, we mustn't allow ourselves to be motivated by such a possibility.

In all probability, good marriages involve mutually providing an audience as a necessary component. Certainly ours does. (I realize that this sounds terribly immodest. So be it.) Neither of us has been notably successful at assembling audiences over the past 32 years in Fort Collins. And as Pat has noted elsewhere, a good self-image is based, at least in part, on what she calls "audience awareness".

Successful people that we have known seem to have in common the unexamined belief that the audience is really out there, and paying attention all the time, and that a superb performance will inevitably be rewarded by a standing ovation (a fire-storm of good, high-quality haptic-acoustical strokes). Linton sensed this in 1936, with his original theatrical definitions of “status” and “role”; also, Goffman's use of “dramaturgical”.

Interpersonal Haptics

One of the major characteristics of human interpersonal communications that determines what response is considered appropriate for a given situation is the “Market

Place" of the strokes being exchanged. The "Market Place" of strokes refers to the emotional price you will pay (or receive) based on the situation. If one is in a high priced market place, one has to pay a much heavier fine for making a mistake. Everyone makes mistakes at various times in their lives, but the emotional Market Place will determine if the mistake is paid for with a "Whoops! I made a mistake", or an "I messed up, and now I have to pay with my life!"

Each family unit, a natural environment for the strong stroke, establishes their own Market Place. One finds that it is much more emotionally stressful to live in a family that has a high market place, and people who come from such families often refuse to admit to ever making a mistake, because the price required for making a mistake is so high that the individual feels that they will not survive. If you have ever met someone (and I think that we all have) who will NEVER admit that they are wrong about ANYTHING, it is likely that they were raised in a high-price emotional market place, and subconsciously they feel that being wrong will result in their execution.

People who have been raised in a low-price emotional market place are usually more calm and tranquil, and less stressful in general. They are allowed to admit that they made a mistake, learn from what they did wrong, and go on with their lives with greater wisdom rather than having to punish themselves unreasonably. It is always healthier and easier to live in a family that has a low-price market place.

Individuals also tend to have a personal emotional market place that can be separate from the exterior family emotional market place. Some people are willing to forgive others for mistakes and not require a heavy emotional penalty, but they will then punish themselves heavily for making a mistake. The most emotionally well-adjusted people will always live in a personal low-price market place, and allow themselves to make a mistake without extracting a heavy penalty.

Sigmund Freud is also renowned for his redefinition of sexual desire as the primary motivational energy of human life. In fact, he attributed all human interaction including that which occurs within the family unit as being sexual in nature on some level of a persons conscious or unconscious mind. There are in fact a wide range of strokes that humans can give each other when interacting, and many of them are not sexual in nature, nor are they motivated by sexual instinct or desire. Although Freud had great insight, his theory of sexuality for the explanation for behavioral motivation doesn't cover the full range of actual human interaction.

A great deal of insight can be gained by looking at the way individuals deal with the transmission of pain. This includes the giving of pain, the accepting of pain and the ignoring of pain. Charles Schultz, the author of the Peanuts comic strip, was a close student of personality types. His depiction of characters illustrates some of the kinds of people that are commonly encountered in life. Some of his more prominent characters include the Lucy (the pain dumper), the Charlie Brown (the pain bearer) and the Snoopy (the pain ignorer.)

As sad as it is unpleasant, we have all encountered Lucys in our lives. Lucys have a strategy of getting attention by being mean and hurtful to the people with whom they interact. Often, these are people with a very poor self-image and/or a broken self-stroker, who have to hurt others and put them down in order to feel good about themselves. They often gravitate to positions of authority so that they are in a position to hurt innocent people because they feel that it eases their own pain and self-loathing in the short run. It is never a good experience to know (or worse yet, be married to) a Lucy. Lucys enjoy watching other people suffer, so slapstick comedy is always funny to them.

The Charlie Brown is the standard pain-bearer personality archetype. The Charlie Brown also generally has a very bad self-image, but also feels that he deserves or are somehow destined to suffer. Charlie Browns resent the Lucys of the world, but they also accept them because they are conditioned to be dumped upon emotionally and bear their own pain as well as that inflicted upon them by other people. Charlie Browns often supplement the pain that is dumped upon them by other people with emotional self-flagellation. It is sometimes possible for a person to become so addicted to emotional pain that he will supply it for himself if there is no one else present to inflict it upon him. The Charlie Brown is by his own definition a loser.

For reasons I can't explain, the Lucy and Charlie Brown personality types are much more commonly encountered in USA and Western culture. Much more rarely, one will meet an individual who is a Snoopy. The Snoopy usually has an excellent self-stroking mechanism, and is not a stroke needer. Snoopys are not dependent upon others for their source of attention and love. When they are dumped upon by a Lucy, they will promptly ignore the flow of emotional pain, and usually conclude that there is something disturbed about the Lucy who has attacked them. They might clearly see that someone they know is a Charlie Brown, but they are also a happy stress-free individual who doesn't have any pain to dump on the pain-bearer. Snoopys will tend to ignore emotional situations as well as the emotional market place, and naturally live in a personal low-price emotional market place, extracting little or no emotional penalty at all for a mistake, either his own, or that of another person. Snoopys frequently come from a family that also maintained a low-price emotional market place, and have been raised with a lot of love, and therefore have a lot of self-confidence and self-love.

The kind of personality type of a given individual is the result of the behavior of their parents. If the individual has a parent who is angry and hurts other people a lot, he is likely to turn in to a Lucy themselves. If his parent or parents are people who suffer a lot, bear the pain of others or inflict emotional pain on themselves, they are more likely to become a Charlie Brown. If a person has emotionally well-adjusted and loving parents, he is likely to be a Snoopy in life. It is a tragedy that so few Snoopys are encountered in American culture. This leads me to believe that there are very few parents who are emotionally healthy, but rather most parents are emotionally twisted in one way or another, so they tend to raise children who are also unhealthy emotionally. Then the cycle repeats itself.

One rule of emotional interaction is that pain always flows down through the social hierarchy. Authoritarians always inflict pain on the people who are subordinate to them. An example of that would be a King who punishes the Captain of the Guard, who then goes home and beats his wife, who in turn spanks her child. The child then kicks the family dog. The sad part of this scenario is that the transmission of pain doesn't really alleviate one's own suffering at all, and at best is a temporary patch. Once one establishes the habit of hurting other people, they become addicted to that behavior, and become an Emotional Vampire. No matter how much of your energy you give to such an individual, they will always want more, because it is not really helping them at all. Sadists are always Lucys, because they thrive on the suffering of other people. A truly healthy family learns to break the cycle of the flow of pain. Living in an emotionally low-price marketplace is one way of accomplishing this.

Intrapersonal Haptics

Evaluating people based on their behavior, one can discern various personality archetypes, denoted by their strategies for survival based upon social interaction. There are many of these personality archetypes in the world, and I will discuss a few noteworthy ones here.

Here are some examples of Personality Archetypes:

The Stroke-Needer: This is someone who has such an impaired ability to love themselves and such a poorly functioning self-stroker that they must depend upon others for love and attention. It is almost always an unpleasant experience to interact with a stroke-needer. A stroke-needer tries to force attention out of other people rather than just allowing themselves to be loved. There are many different strategies to get attention employed by different kinds of stroke-needers.

Mrs. Greenthumb is a gardening expert who occasionally appeared on the Regis and Kelly show. She is a hyperactive individual with a raucous voice and a nervous energy that creates a display which sucks the energy out of the viewer. She jumps around like a hysterical idiot and appears to be too energetic as a means of attracting attention. A person who truly has a lot of energy can be uplifting to watch, but when it is insincere, it can be draining to the audience.

Don S. is a very unintelligent person who wants desperately to be seen as a smart person. He invited himself into my parents' book club, where in fact no one wanted him. The book club consisted of ex-professors and their wives, except for Don S. who insinuated himself into this club without the willing endorsement of the other members. He liked to see himself as an intellectual, where in fact he was actually an investment councilor.

Jack C's life is pretence. Like many stroke-needers, he wants to be seen as being a smart person. He sends Christmas cards intended to display how clever he is. In addition to being an uncontrolled braggart, he tries to appear popular when he is not. He is a photographer, and sends pictures of people he doesn't even know to make it look as if he has a lot of friends.

Cynthia B. was one of my father's students at CSU. She was a very large and overweight lady who sought attention by playing the outraged card. She would rant on about injustices in the world in an attempt to get other people's feathers ruffled over causes she was upset about, usually

related to the plight of the Native American Indians. She learned that people went out of their way to avoid her, so she learned to hide at the ends of the isles in the supermarket and ambush her potential audience.
Barbra P. was another shameless bragger. She would brag about events which had not yet happened in order to get the "Wow! You are so cool!" stroke. She went on about a novel which she planned to write in the future, so she could collect the desired strokes in advance. Her daughter was newly hired to a company which she insisted that her daughter would some day be the head of. She also thought of herself as being very smart, and wanted other people to see her as being very smart too, even though the only events she had to brag about had not yet occurred

Phyllis M. was a strange lady who, once she had one's attention, was almost impossible to get away from. She was full of bizarre stories which she thought were very clever. In one of these tales she offered some workmen coffee and realized that she was out of cream when she got into her kitchen. She claims that she then milked her own breasts into the cream pitcher (she was lactating at the time) and served it to the unsuspecting workers. She was always filled with stories to dazzle and amaze her audience in order to get attention and strokes.

My (Curtis) ex-wife JoAnn appeared on the outside to be a Lucy. She constantly nagged me and spoke in a harsh tone of voice. She played childish practical jokes on me (like putting tacks in my shoes) and would laugh when she succeeded at hurting me. She was critical and did her best to tear down my ego; she would control the finances (although I made a majority of the money) and did her best to cut me off from my friends and family. Even though she never physically assaulted me, she displayed every other kind of abusive behavior that typifies an Emotional Vampire. In reality, she was very insecure and had a terrible self-image. She was not capable of supplying herself with love, and didn't know how to go about getting it from me, so in frustration she would resort to being mean. On a subconscious level, she thought that she could bully love out of me. Every time she gave me an angry look or spoke to me in a harsh tone, it made me love her a little less. She also liked to play the "crazy card" which was as effective at sucking out my energy as being mean and angry. In the end, she ended up divorced for a third time, and I barely escaped the marriage with my life and sanity.

I had a friend in 5th grade named Jeff Lanm who was beaten terribly by his drunken ex-Hell's Angels biker mother. She would take a belt to him for little or no reason, and was rarely seen fully dressed. Not surprisingly, Jeff (who was only 10 years old) had more pain than he could bear, so seeing another person in pain was delightful to him. Whenever I got hurt, he could not help but to laugh out loud. He would cause dangerous situations because he wanted to see me hurt. He also would "accidentally" break or destroy things almost every time we played together, to see how much he could get forgiven for. The more infractions he would be forgiven for, the more he felt he was cared about. This is not an unusual behavior for people who are desperate stroke needers.

The Joker: I myself (Curtis) fit into this category. I have spent much of my life making people laugh with my jokes. I felt that I was bringing bliss to people, and I enjoyed making people happy. I would fall down, eat paper, act silly, and do absurd things, all in an attempt to get attention. Although this was fun and succeeded at getting attention, I realize in retrospect that this behavior didn't earn me any respect. Further, women rarely want to date a clown, so the sacrifice was not worth the benefit.

The Pseudo-Diva: This person craves the "you are such a wonderful musician!" stroke, even though they usually have no talent at all, and frequently cannot distinguish one note from another. They usually own at least one instrument, and often seek music lessons, which are mostly wasted. They culture the appearance of a musician and tell everyone how great they are. Their actual performances are excruciating to hear.

The Pseudo-Guru: This person lives for and is addicted to the "Life is like a well" stroke. The continually spout words of wisdom which are generally meaningless. They wish to be thought of as wise, where they are actually an egotist with no real wisdom to impart.

One might wonder why there are so many kinds of stroke-needers in American culture. I believe that too many families establish an unhealthy high-price emotional market place, but further, our system of human interaction doesn't leave enough contexts where love is appropriate. I think that American WASP culture inherited this from English and European Puritan culture, both of which are stuffy and impersonal on an emotional level, as well as employing very high-price emotional market places. Just because one's culture teaches something does not necessarily make it right. My advice to everyone is that they rely on their own heart and perceptions to help them decide how to be kind and decent to other people, and try to rise above the stressful behaviors which they have inherited from their family and culture.

The Authoritarian: This is one of the most dangerous kinds of people. With little exception, authoritarians are people who subconsciously feel that they are weak. Because of this, they seek power and want to be seen as powerful. They like to feel as though they have power, and love to exercise their power over their subordinates. They usually have a poor self-stroking mechanism, and are almost always Lucys. This kind of person almost always gravitates towards positions of power, but abuses it when it is attained. They have an almost magnetic attraction to any Charlie Brown in the vicinity, and are often sadistic in nature, enjoying the suffering of other people. This kind of person frequently seeks a vocation in the law enforcement or corrections fields, so that they can harm others and make it seem normal and acceptable. Since authoritarians are emotional vampires, no amount of life force they suck out of other people will ever satiate their hunger. They are like a bottomless well that can never be filled. They tend to suck life out of their victims until their victims die of cancer or some other psychosomatic disease, after which they then seek out another victim. It is impossible to satiate the lust of an authoritarian for the suffering of human beings. Authoritarians are also frequently cowards, thus they tend to cluster together and attack helpless people in a group (police being an excellent example here.) A brave person is not bothered by facing an enemy alone. An authoritarian on the other hand verifies that the battle has already been won before they attack their victim. Other examples of authoritarians include school supervisors, managers, bullies, judges, military personnel, district attorneys, state troopers and frequently politicians.

The Motor-mouth: This is a person who is desperately afraid that the person they are talking to is going to say something that will hurt their feelings, so they never shut up or take a breath, or let anyone else enter then conversation or make a comment of their own.

The Materialistic Possessor: This is a shallow individual who tries to collect strokes because they have fancy possessions, a big house or an expensive new car, for example.

The Promiser: This person promises to do favors and collects the gratitude in advance. This kind of person never comes through on the promises he makes; he just wants credit and gratitude for making the offer.

The Pseudo-Friend: This kind of person is usually a rogue and/or a thief. Pseudo-friends pretend to be your friend in order to get invited inside of your house, but they literally steal money and/or valuables from you every time they come inside. They are not really a friend at all, and their sole goal is to rip you off for as much as they can get. Sometimes they are actually a businessperson of some kind, who pretends to be your friend in order to sell you something or get you involved in inadvisable business deals.

The Aggressive Squid: An interpersonal tactic which consists of attacking suddenly and without warning, and then scuttling behind a screen (or cloud of ink) in order to be protected against counterattack. This is a tactic commonly employed by Lucys. It has the advantage of allowing one to hurt his victim without risking being hurt himself.

The Fairy Princess: Another personal matrix, this one designating an individual who expects and demands special privileges, considerations, courtesies, etc. A Fairy Princess can be of either gender. Among contemporary USians, this is most commonly found in young, thin, pretty women, the stock from which come high fashion models and beauty contest winners. Culturally, they are defined as winners long before they enter their first contest. (But, see GLAMOUR-PUSS for a down-side version of this one.)

The Little-Old-Lady-In-A-Wheel-Chair: One member of the inventory of personal strategies generated by this theory; in this instance, the individual who attacks another, and defends her/himself against counterattack by appearing so vulnerable that no responsible person would DREAM of hitting her/him back. People who play this role are always Lucys.

Note that a majority of personality types use strategies to get love and attention that trick, force or punish energy out of other people. It would appear that a healthy person would allow themselves to be loved and not need to resort to deceptive strategies in order to get the attention they crave.

However, actual personalities are not always so clearly defined. Most people can play the role of a Charlie Brown when they feel bad about themselves. When a person is feeling very happy and good about themselves, they are more likely to display the characteristics of a Snoopy. Almost everyone can be a Lucy when they are really angry, but obviously there are many ways to deal with anger. A Charlie Brown frequently takes his anger out on himself, rather than inflicting it on someone else the way a Lucy does.

A healthy strategy for surviving in any emotional market place is to be aware of the different roles people play, and simply refuse to be a part of it. Most of people's behavior is learned and then ingrained through continued use over a period of years and/or decades. It is important to learn to not cause one's self harm, and to have the self-respect to not bear pain for other people. It is important to learn to deal with one's own pain without having to inflict it upon other people. It is a sign of good character to be able to show kindness to others even one is in great pain, and to stand up to the Lucys of the world when they target you as their victim.

I think that it is also worthy to mention that the simple presence of another person is an important haptic experience, even if and when they are not interacting with one another. A couple who is closely bonded emotionally can experience this wonderful haptic sensation if they are just watching a movie, sleeping in the same bed or just enjoying a beautiful sunset together. Talking or touching physically does not have to be a part of the feeling for it to be a powerful sensation. Similarly, a child might feel safer and happier just knowing that one or both of their parents are home, just knowing that this is the case often as an effect on the child's feelings.

Chapter 8: The Haptics of Communication

When closely examining American English, one finds that in virtually all dialects, a huge amount of the terminology used refers to the human body, both internally and externally. This applies even more to metaphors. When using words to colorfully refer to other people and the environment in a non-literal way, many of the metaphorical terms are bodily related.

To illustrate this point, I am going to go through a Metaphor Exercise. This exercise lists various parts of the body, and associated metaphors. These metaphors are examples of terms that refer to the human body internally:

HEADS: a hole in the head, to give head, gone to his head, fat head, to come to a head, to head off, ahead of the game, to put a head on it, to get up a head of steam, to head up, to head toward, to head off, to head in

EYES: shifty-eyed, wide-eyed, squinty-eyed, keen-eyed, beady-eyed, to eyeball, "a wink is a good as a nod", "to fish-eye", eye of the storm, bull's eye

NOSES: a brown-nose, nosey, turn up your nose, poke your nose in, to nose around, (operations): it stinks, rotten idea, rotten apple, fetid, sweet smell of success, "come up smelling like a rose", snort, sniff

MOUTHS: a mouthy person, to mouth off, down in the mouth, the mouth of the river, big mouth, mouth of the cannon (volcano, mineshaft, tunnel), leave a bad taste in the mouth, TEETH: in the teeth of the evidence, in the teeth of the storm, a sweet tooth, toothsome, fangs for the memories, bit in my teeth, sink your teeth into it, set you teeth on edge, long in the tooth, grit your teeth, to chew the fat, to bite the bullet, LIPS: don't give me no lip, throw a lip over it, to lip-read, lip-diddling, loose-lipped, liver-lipped, Bronx cheer, licking his chops, the raspberry, white-lipped and trembling, JAWS: jaws of a wrench, of a vice, of pliers, jawing, snatch victory from the jaws of defeat, jaws of doom, set your jaw, dropped his jaw, slack-jawed, CHIN: keep your chin up, to chin, TONGUE: silver tongued, "the tongue is a fire", to give tongue (an obsolete British slang term; not what it sounds like), wagon tongue, tongue of a shoe

MOUTH OPERATIONS: It's too hard to swallow, "I wouldn't spit on his shoes", all oral intercourse humor, "it sucks", (1960s bumper-sticker: "There is no gravity; the earth sucks!"), vomiting humor, to catch your breath, a sip, "don't hold your breath", the sweet taste of victory, a taste of Utopia, bitter disappointment, spicy sex, sour expression, salty talk, to blow (various meanings), to blow off, to blow out, to blow in, to blow up, to blow down

THROATS: shoving it down my throat, deep throat, golden throat, lump in the throat, easy to swallow, he'll swallow anything, goes down easy, swallowed it hook, line, and sinker, catch in the throat, to cough it up, to choke on it
NECK: neck of a bottle, pain in the neck, to neck (kiss), neck and neck, stick your neck out

LUNGS: don't breathe a word, like a breath of fresh air, it took my breath away, it was a breath of Spring, it breathed an air of mystery, with his last breath, it was a breathless moment, lung power, black lung, I can breathe easy again, don't hold your breath

HEARTS: sick at heart, my heart stood still, my heart leapt up, a warm heart, cold-hearted, soft-hearted, hard-hearted, the heart of the matter, give your heart away, a stolen heart, your cheatin' heart, with high heart, makes my heart bleed, a broken heart, heart-throb, in my heart, sweet heart, dear heart, true- hearted, my heart sang (danced), loving heart, evil-hearted, heart of stone, lion-hearted, chicken-hearted

STOMACHS: I can't stomach that, to belly-ache, to digest the argument, to have a belly-full, to belly up to the bar, belly- up, "it turned my stomach", "I had a gut-ful", to "guts-it", gut-level feeling, busted a gut, he has guts, gutty guy, pain in the gut, (fire) gutted the house, butterflies in the stomach

LIVERS: liverish, lily-livered

GENITALS :(The entire corpus of Freudian symbolism, for openers!)
(How about Cabell, Jurgen?), the Indian tradition of Lingam and Yoni, that Australian aboriginal culture hero, the Foolish One of the Mandan, (standard folklore sources), Maledicta, small penis and large vagina jokes, large penis jokes ("Schultz is dead!"), impotence jokes (limp noodle, limber dick, "those aren't fruit flies; your banana died"), sexual insatiability of women jokes, gay and lesbian humor, masturbation humor, ethnic jokes, bestiality jokes, anal intercourse jokes ("I don't see any WHEELS"), "fuck off!", to "fuck up", to "fuck the dog", to "fuck over", "fucked out", "fuck you!", "shove it up your ass!", get shafted

LARGE INTESTINES AND ANUSES: Hageseth, Mark Twain, outhouse jokes, all farting humor (to cut a cheese, break wind, pass gas, toot, coarsen the atmosphere, float an air bubble), shit-head, shit face, don't give a shit, tough shit, hot shit, fulla shit, the various species of shit (horse-, bull-, chicken-, ape-, dog-, whale-, cat-, bat-, sheep, pig-, bird-, all nursery euphemisms (doo doo, noonie, poo poo, etc.), droppings, manure jokes, enema humor

BODY FLUIDS: BLOOD: hot-blooded, cold-blooded, "blood is thicker than water", menstrual blood jokes and curses (from British "bloody" to Sambia male terror) URINE: to be "pissed off" (USian), to be "pissed" (British), to "piss away", a "piss-ant", a "piss-willy", PERSPIRATION: "no sweat", to "sweat it out" (two senses), to "sweat blood", "the sweat of your brow", TEARS: "blood, sweat, and tears" (Churchill), the Romantic tear, SALIVA: to spit on, to spit up, to spit in the wind, "spit in the ocean" {poker}, SEMEN: to "come", oral sex jokes

This second part of this metaphor exercise is similar to the first, this time listing external bodily references:

Various metaphoric extensions of "TO TOUCH" - "touchy", "to be touched", "Midas touch", "out of touch", "in touch with", "reach out and touch somebody", "light touch", "wouldn't touch it with a ten-foot pole"

Symbolic extensions of synonyms for "touching": "grabbing", "grasping", "gripping", "manipulation", "holding", "pinching", "hitting", "stroking", "petting" and "pets", "scratching", "put me down", "jerk me around", "shook me up", "that tickles me", "a ticklish situation", "it rattled me", "it moved me", "I was really touched", "don't push me around", "a slap in the face", "uplifted", to "good in the clutch", "put one on hold", "pinch pennies", "feel out of it", "I feel for you", "get the feel of it", "I feel ......" (experience emotions, or internal sensations)

Symbolic extensions of the HAND: symbol of whole person, applause, guilty participation, maintaining a skill level, card-playing, "handouts", "hand-me-downs", "with folded hands", "hands across the ocean", right hand vs. left hand, protection and nurturance, fairness, capture, "hot hand", "cool hand", "cold hands, warm heart", "glad-hand", "hand-in-glove", "hand-in- hand", "hand-over-fist"; "handsome", "glad-hander", "handyman", "high-handed", "upper hand", "under-handed", "back-hand", "at hand", "ham-handed", "hand-made", "red-handed", "Black Hand", "hands down", "my hands are tied", "handle", "get a handle on it", "four-in-hand", "overhand", "handkerchief", "right hand man", open-handed

FISTS: "close-fisted", "iron fist in a velvet glove"

FINGERS: "finger of fate", "the moving finger", "a finger in the pie", to examine the merchandise, to identify a criminal, “butter-fingers”, "light-fingered", THUMBS: to "thumb" a ride, to thumb the nose, "thumb-fingered", "thumbs up" "green thumb", "under your thumb"; INDEX FINGER: to point, to "point", to make a point, to poke or prod, to indicate; LITTLE FINGER: teacups and water in the ear; RING FINGER: the label indicates the symbolism; MIDDLE FINGER: The Los Angeles Freeway Salute, Danny Kaye in "The Inspector General"

WRISTS: sports, music, "getting your wrist into it"

ARMS: "long arm of the Law", "short arm", "coat of arms", "at arm's length", army, armor, armory, "straight-arm", disarm

LEGS AND FEET: "not a leg to stand on", "legging it", "bootlegger", "daddy-long-legs", "foot in the mouth", "manure-foot", "light-footed", "a foot in the door", "step up", "step down", "step in ", "step out", "stomp", "marching to a different drummer", "stumble", "skip", "tramp", "kick", "boot", "ramble", to "tap- dance", various "kick" phrases

TOES: "toe the mark", "toe the line", "dip your toe in", "twinkle-toes", "turn up his toes", "on your toes", "to tiptoe"

BACKS: "get his back up", "get off my back", "back to the wall", "back off"

FACES: to lose face, to face it bravely, to face the storm, the face of the mountain, in your face, a slap in the face, to face off (hockey), poker face, face like a clenched fist, to save face

HAIR: the hair of the dog, a hairy situation, the short hairs, a hair-raising experience, hairy-chested, hair-ball

This list is by no means comprehensive. As a fun exercise, try coming up with bodily related metaphors yourself. You might be surprised at how many you can think of!

Human speech reflects how people see and relate to life itself. If the aforementioned metaphorical terms are a measure of how humans relate to life, it appears that the experience of being in a human body, and the haptics thereof, play a major role in the way humans perceive the world around them.

Chapter 9: Haptic Theory as it Applies to Religion

I see and wish to bring attention to a link between traditional Christian theology and social science theory. Most social scientists and anthropologists are either atheists or agnostic, or if they are religionists, they don't see any relevance between their professional work and their religious convictions. This chapter will take a look at how Christians have learned to conceive God, social science theory as it has developed over the last century, and finally a new theoretical approach in the social sciences which has the potential of avoiding the error of avoiding religion, as most major theorists have.

The traditional images of God are that of an anthropomorphized being who appears in human form. From Genesis 1:1: God was in human form and walked with Adam in the Garden of Eden. One quote from the bible states, "And God turned his face from the children of Israel." On the ceiling of the Sistine Chapel, God is depicted in human form in *Creation of Adam* by Michelangelo. In Rembrandt's *Belshazzar's Feast*, the handwriting on the wall is being made by the hand of God. One quote from Handel's *Messiah* is, "The mouth of the Lord has spoken it." Finally the Bible states that "Man was created in God's image." Clearly, Christians have been raised to believe that God looks like a man in appearance.

Why these images of God in human form? Many Christians take this concept of God in human form as being literal, but it is also possible that it is meant to be seen as symbolic. These corporeal metaphors are intended to remind us of the nature of the communicative events that link us to God. The scriptures tell us that God walks and talks to us. He hears us and gives gifts to us. He sends angels and other spirits to us, and he receives our prayers. He keeps track of what we mortals are doing, collectively as well as individually (having first practiced this sort of spiritual accounting with the children of Israel.) God was seen as the institutor of a universal moral order by the prophets of the Old Testament. To the ancient Israelite authors of the various books of the Old Testament, it made supreme sense that a God who communicated as humans do would be endowed with a selected set of human features. (We might note in passing that other ancient religions utilized a different set of anatomical metaphors for their deities: the Lingam and Yoni in traditional Hindu iconography, for example.) And, of course, the supreme image of the New Testament is that of God made Man, in the person of Christ. It is through Christ that we communicate with God, which is made possible by the fact that God was made Flesh, and dwelt among us.

The social sciences grew up during the 19th century. Held roundly in tandem by their common focus on human behavior (both past and current), their common goal was the application of the perspective of science to the description and ultimate understanding of the Human Condition. Diverse in subject matter, they struggled to develop a common theoretical perspective which might provide a basis for synthesizing their various findings. For most of the theorists of that century, the success that Darwinian evolution had achieved in the biological sciences, and building on the notion of the social evolution derived from the French philosophies of the 18th century, these thinkers proved the newly emerging knowledge of the ancient human past for clues to solve the mighty mystery of the ancient birth of humanity. They were collectively obsessed with the question of how it all started. Having rejected the traditional scriptural account of our common beginnings, they speculated about the manner and conditions of our rise to human status. Naturally, they were uniquely human features such as language, kinship, politics and the like. Now, I am not going into detail as to the various theories and theorists of that period; there are too many of them, and they are not all of equal importance. I will briefly mention two theorists, possibly the most creative of the period, and certainly the most influential, in terms of the long and wide-ranging impact and consequences of their theories.

Karl Marx (and his side-kick Friedrich Engels) created "dialectical materialism", a theory of society which saw the ultimate origin of all things human in the material circumstances of life. Marx saw the carburetor of history as the Class Struggle, the inevitable conflict between the wealthy and powerful (who controlled society and its institutions for their own benefit), and the poor working classes, exploited and abused, locked in perpetual poverty, squalor and hopelessness. Marx had little interest in religion, dismissing it scornfully as the "opiate of the masses", assuming that organized religion was merely a part of the conspiracy of the Powerful designed to keep the Poor industrious and apathetic. Neither Marx nor Engels were anthropologists, and consequently had little knowledge of nor interest in non-European peoples and cultures.

Sigmund Freud, the other theoretical giant of the 19th century, best known as the father of Psychoanalysis, built his theories of the Human Experiences on the development of the individual psyche, with particular reference to the ways in which this development could go wrong, resulting in psychological miseries in adulthood. Freud saw religion as neurosis, a symptom of a disturbed personality, with the implication that the truly sane, adult individual would have no need for religious faith or convictions.

There were other theorists of religion, disagreeing in major ways about its nature, origins, and utility, but sharing the basic conviction that religion was, at best, an afterthought to the more important dimensions of human life.

Are we, then, stuck with the melancholy conclusion that religion is either irrelevant to the serious concerns of life, or else the product of human irrationality? This is not my view. I see emerging from advances in knowledge in many different disciplines, across the spectrum of the sciences and humanities, a new theoretical approach which has the potential to correct the errors of earlier theories, and to open new opportunities for understanding our common humanity, and for dealing more effectively with the common problems and threats which we face as a species. An important byproduct of this new approach may well be the restoration of religion to a place of central concern in social theory and social practice.

The Haptic Approach takes a viewpoint emerging from work in several different fields of scientific endeavor, principally during the past three decades.

Conventional accounts of primate evolution tend to neglect the sense of touch. Primates, with their clever hands, traffic with their environments in ways that are distinctive from those of other mammalian creatures and species. In particular, primates' modes of feeding, locomotion, and intra-group communication differ in revolutionary ways from those of other mammalian species.

The hominid hand, clearly one of the triumphs of evolution, uniquely combines keen sensory input with unparalleled abilities not only to manipulate objects precisely and more large masses efficiently, but also, to execute complex series of operations directed toward the accomplishment of goals (algorithms.)

The hominid mouth, far from being merely a convenient ingress and egress for solids, liquids, and gasses, is, in its own right, a major traffic area for vocal signals, affectional and erotic message, and a supplementary area for the manipulation of objects.

Our subjective awareness, in contrast with our internal experiences, contains a major component of haptic messaging. The assertion here is that subjective awareness is "Touch-like", rather than "speech-like" or "sight-like". And while it may be legitimately argued that verbal messages play a part in subjective information processing, this aspect has generally been over-emphasized by psychologists.

Subjective haptic messaging systems must operate at least as fast as the external realization of cerebral commands. Consider, if you will, the complexity and rapidity of subjective information-processing that takes place while a pianist is performing the opening bars of Beethoven's *Pathetique* Sonata in front of a concert audience. If this information were coded verbally and spoken (aloud or silently), it would undoubtedly take several minutes to perform, instead of the few brief seconds required by the original performance.

Or, to take a somewhat more accessible example, consider a similar situation involving an NFL quarterback, with his team trailing, facing fourth and long in the closing seconds of the game. He takes the snap from the center, deftly avoids a five-man blitz, reads his down-field coverages, and fires a perfect strike to his wide-out for the game-winning score. As in the case of the concert pianist, the complexity and speed of the subjective decision-making processes would require minutes of verbal recital, in contrast to those five seconds or so of elapsed time of the original play.

Our ancestors did not become human in one fell swoop. Their trajectory towards humanity was a piecework process, and in the final result was an assemblage of trends of different historical depths and precedents. Thus, "magic moment" theories, which posit discontinuity in the evolutionary process, are fatally flawed.

Our best perspective on the pre-human condition is provided by the African apes, who display at least two kinds of manual algorithms: technological (construction of termiting sticks), and interpersonal (grooming, hitting, and threatening.)

The emergence of language among our earliest hominid

ancestors was the result of the transfer of manual algorithms to the mouth, as the hands became more intensely involved in creating and recreating the world of experience through the new domain of artifacts.

Language consists of acoustical symbols, arranged in certain conventional ways. It is argued that all symbols are haptic in nature and origin, and that all verbal utterances arise from a sort of haptic "deep structure", the locus of those haptic algorithms, both technological and interpersonal, which we inherited from our pre-hominid ancestors and elaborated during the hominid trajectory.

The basis for the bald assertion that all symbols are haptic in nature lies in the notion that symbols map the world into distinct entities, with sharp boundaries and distinctive contents. Some symbols are contained in bounded sets (color terminologies, kin-term sets), others are not; however, all assume boundedness. We are able to sort the world into sharply bounded entities with symbolic representation because we were first able to sort objects into groups with our hands.

Not all symbols were created equal. Major symbols (which impact millions of lives), retain their basic haptic character, in that they both a) point to, or indicate something, and b) convey a powerful emotional impact; i.e. they have the power to move people (sometimes in opposite directions.) Think, for example, of the Christian Cross, or the Berlin Wall. The fact that they have become major symbols is undoubtedly related both to the complexity and saliency of the semantic packages to which they point, and their power to impact their consumers.

If there is any validity to the foregoing, it has some interesting implications.

There is a new perspective on the arts. We need no longer see these activities and products as either the outcomes of subterranean psychic forces and entities, or alternatively, as the reflections of economic forces and relations. It makes more sense to see the creating of art as the realization of important algorithms and heuristics which pervade daily life.

Music, in particular, is seen as the product of human mouths and hands (and manually constructed sounds generators), which translate internalized programs into acoustical performances (Lomax, 1976, provides the background for this discussion.) Skillfully made music provides something else which is cherished in every known human society, the virtuoso display of clever hands and mouths. Presumably, dancing provides similar rewards, differing only in that entire bodies are on display.

“Personality”, a term so widely used, and yet, maddeningly elusive in definition, becomes, in this framework, the total input-output matrix of the haptic signals and messages of an individual, qualified by the further observation that the individual can both send and receive haptic messages to and from his/herself.

Social systems become the basic matrices of external haptic messaging systems. “Status” and “role” become locus and exchange parameters of haptic messages. Kinship systems remain of substantial interest, because of their comprehensive nature in many traditional societies, and because of their crucial function in socialization.

Religion, from this viewpoint, is based on our earliest haptic experiences of the world, amplified and modified by our later experiences with individuals and groups (the family being the most important, and embodying the most important heuristics and algorithms of our cultures (technological, interpersonal, artistic, economic, etc.) “Secular” societies (unusually urban, industrial, and depersonalized) are generally societies which have convictions and have been driven underground (Poland, during the last 40 years, for example.)

The deepest, most profound sense of the orderliness of the world will be codified in a people's communal sense of the Divine. And possibly the most enlightened sense of cosmic orderliness will include the realization that "all roads lead to the top of the mountain", and that all peoples are seeking enlightenment in their own way, and have a right to do so.

Chapter 10: The Haptics of Musical Performance

Music-making is accomplished through the use of haptic monitors (the sense of touch) in conjunction with acoustical monitors (the sense of hearing.)

Every instrument has its own haptic requirements, which must be painfully mastered.

Becoming a virtuoso pianist, or any other kind of artistic mastery, is an excellent example of the difference between algorithms as opposed to heuristics. When one learns to play an instrument, they use exercises that familiarize the student with the instrument, develop manual dexterity, and teach them the scales (modes) in which music of their culture is written. Playing scales and exercises is an algorithmic activity. However, once mastery of an instrument is achieved, the performance takes on a very different quality. As a true virtuoso performs in public, he tunes each note individually based on acoustical feedback, and often tailor the phrases for the room in which she is playing and/or the specific audience for whom they are performing. Therefore, playing a concerto superbly is a heuristic.

Each family of instruments has its own haptic requirements.

Brass instruments are primarily involved with the conjunction of acoustical signal-processing and haptic signals from the mouth muscles or bilabial "embouchure", teeth, and tongue (and only trivially with signals from the fingers and arm muscles), plus careful control of breathing.

Woodwinds are generally similar to the brasses; however, the embouchures are more various. Flute embouchures involve producing a direct air stream which crosses the hole in the mouthpiece transversely; the single reed embouchure uses single lip pressure on the bottom of the reed to control the sound; the double reed embouchure uses bilabial pressure to control both reeds.

The string instruments involve a similar conjunction between acoustical signals and haptic signals from the fingertips and the receptors within the finger, arm, and shoulder muscles. The violin family, which unlike the guitar is fretless, depends heavily on the heuristic feedback of the coordination of the exact placement of the fingers and the acoustical feedback of hearing to fine-tune every note to an excruciating level of precision. This family might possibly be the most difficult to play in the world.

Like the strings, the percussion instruments involve finger and hand monitors, but unlike the strings, most percussion instruments are concerned with movements of the entire hand, and forearm, rather than just the fingers. The percussion instruments, in other words, are played with the power grip as well as the precision grip. A drummer must have the ability to hold to the rhythm of the musical script precisely, where a true percussionist (who might be called on to play the timpani) also has to be able to use acoustical feedback to play in tune with the rest of the orchestra.

Acoustical keyboards such as the piano-forte require much more haptic feedback than electronic keyboards or harpsichords. A piano will produce various volume levels based on how fast the key is struck. A skilled pianist is also in control of how long the note will reverberate, and has facility with various dynamics and accents. Electronic keyboards are similar to a harpsichord in that the keyboardist depresses keys, but the sound is produced electronically and or mechanically, and the accent and dynamics do not require or provide as much control as does a piano. The harpsichord is a very early and basic keyboard instrument, which gives the player almost no control over the volume dynamic. However, an electronic keyboard gives the musician a wide range of synthesized sounds that he can produce. The amount of haptic and acoustical feedback that is required to play any instrument is proportionate to the range of sounds which that instrument is capable of producing.

The voice as a musical instrument is more involved with haptic feedback than any other instrument. Since the voice is part of the performers body, the vibrations generated by the tones are felt inside the body, especially the part of the face called the "singing mask" From top to bottom this extends to a line just above the eyebrows, down to just above the upper lip and side to side from hairline to hairline. In the lower pitches called the "chest register" the vibrations can be felt in the chest. As the singer strives for higher and higher pitches the vocal chords stretch longer and this can also be felt. Unlike other instruments in which the performer can see what his/her fingers are doing, the singer has to rely entirely on this haptic feedback and the sound. Another way in which the voice differs from other instruments is that only one musician can play any given instrument (the voice he was born with.) This instrument will change from time to time depending on the physical condition of the performer. But the major difference is that the singer's performance includes lyrics. The singer must become an actor, portraying various characters in various situations and moods and must become skillful at communicating strokes to the audience through his/ her body language, facial expressions and the use of a variety of tone colors which the other instruments can't begin to achieve.

The musical manuscript is detailed, yet incomplete, in that "playing the notes" does not guarantee a satisfactory performance. Information is contained in both digital and analogue instructions. Pitches and sequences are digital; meter, tempo, variable speed, and dynamics are analogical.

Chapter 11: The Haptics of America and the Rest of the World

One of the most defining characteristics of the United States of America is the ecology of mindless waste. Not only has the economy of America become dependant upon the ravenous consumption of natural resources, but that consumption is frequently unnecessary. A huge amount of natural rainforest is cut down every day (rainforest being an essential part of the world ecology), and a majority of the paper is used for the absurd packaging of fast food. We in America then produce more garbage than any other country in the world. The manner of packaging of this nutritionless food is often wasteful and inefficient. I have seen handfuls of napkins thrown immediately into the garbage without being used. I have seen single burgers wrapped in multiple layers of packaging. The use of Styrofoam is shameful. Just today I ordered biscuits and gravy with the gravy in a separate container, and rather than wrapping the biscuits in paper they placed two dry biscuits in a huge Styrofoam container, completely unnecessarily. The amount of mindless waste and production of garbage in America is truly amazing! America also produces a huge amount of toxic waste that is then dumped into the environment. This practice is one of the final nails in the coffin of the world's ecology that will lead to the total collapse of the Earth's biosphere.

A trend in the USA over the last three decades is the quest for sensory intensity. We are producing hotter, spicier foods, louder music, more violent movies, sexier clothing and more graphically violent video games than ever before. America has often been referred to as a "melting pot" of the various cultures of immigrants coming from every country on the Earth. As a result, one can find restaurants that specialize in cuisine from hundreds of different countries. Further, people are becoming increasingly lazy when it comes to the cooking of their own food. Fifty years ago people were much more likely to cook their own meals from scratch, where now on top of the huge variety of frozen and prepared dinners available, many restaurant foods are available for delivery or carry-out. Rather that doing the work themselves, people waste money so that they can get their food prepared for them, and then the food is packaged in ways that create additional waste with the inefficient packaging.

Part of this gastronomic explosion intensity of taste is the wide variety of cooking shows that turn cooking in the house into a performance art. Emeril, Rachael Ray and many other TV cooks allow people to learn new cooking techniques and recipes so that they can provide delicious extravagant meals for their guests and families. There is nothing wrong with this, but the point being that modern technology allows for a much more diverse experience of sensation in life.

The internet has now become the vastest resource of information in the history of the world. Once upon a time, people relied on recipes they invented or were handed down through their family, shared between friends, or in a cookbook. One's library of cookbooks was heavily relied on, where now anyone with the internet has a vast number of recipes available on demand. There are dozens of web sites with cooking recipes, and hundreds of recipes on each one. I own one cookbook, but I can find any recipe I want (and variations of each one) on the internet.

Another trend in America since the 1960's is the broadening of sexual mores. Homosexuality on the part of both genders has become much more accepted generally, to the point that being gay or bisexual has become glamorous in some environments. And a large number of people (of a variety of sexual orientations) hold an appreciation for gorgeous, hot, young sexy lesbian couples.

The American family unit has become much more polymorphous than it was back in the conformist 1950's. The traditional American family unit used to consist of two parents (man and wife) and two or more children (many couples would shoot for at least one of each gender.) Now the single parent family unit has become almost an epidemic, particularly in financially poor communities. With women getting pregnant at a young age and out of wedlock, the grandparent – grandchildren family has also become more common. This commonly is caused because girls who have a baby when they are in high school are usually too young to be able to financially support their child. Although it is still prohibited in many states, the family unit with same-sex parents is also becoming more prevalent. People used to adhere to strict traditional American values when forming family units. The rule in America is that any family unit that is financially viable is good.

TIME magazine published an article about convergence of hard core porn and legitimate films. American film makers have been more and more willing to show increasingly sexually explicit scenes in movies of all rating levels. It is now accepted throughout American culture that the internet, while it is used for all forms of recreation and business, is primarily used for sexual purposes. All forms of trans-sexuality and transvestitism have been greatly enhanced by the use of the internet and major advancements in technology.

Sex and violence has also seen a dramatic up rise in the last few decades. As the pain level in America has risen (especially since the year 2000), sexual and violent acts against children has gone up enormously. The number of sexual stalkers has been on the rise over the last forty years. There has also been a rise in cults and bizarre forms of sexual contact, including vampiristic sex and sloshing (sex including food.)

The Mass Media has made it possible for people to indulge in a huge amount of sensation in many forms. Movies and a vast number of entertaining activities are available over the internet, which has now shifted from dial-up modems using lines that were designed for analog transmission to high-speed broadband connections which are getting faster every year using dedicated digitals lines like fiber-optics.

A sad but very real development has been the loss of childhood innocence. We now have rising requirements for all levels of education - entry requirements and graduation ceremonies for kindergarten curriculum vitae and performance folders for toddlers. Children are now pushed harder than ever to set goals of Olympic and professional goals and a very young age. Sex, drugs and violence are now more a part of children's lives at a younger age than ever. The internet now makes pornography available to any child who can access their parent's computer and credit card. One can see that more and more frequently Television has become a resource for education of the young. Guns have become highly accessible to people of all ages. The collective American psyche feels the loss of innocence of our young; the use of young girls in current day commercials could be seen as nostalgia for lost innocence.

America has also suffered from a general loss of consensus. The politicizing of the public schools has made our educational system a forum for debates over the teaching of sex education, curriculum and the abuse of drugs. People's personal sexual morality has also been made a matter of political debate, such as the regulation and prohibition of gay marriage. There are now interest groups for anything and everything. The last eight years of illegal politics have cast a very poor shadow upon the conservative WASP population of America, who used to have the nerve to call themselves the "moral majority."

Finally, the internet now allows a form of electronic cocooning in which individuals generate social groups to associate with purely over the internet, while rarely venturing out into the world. We can now even order our meals over the internet and have them delivered right to our front door. It is now possible to buy almost any product one can need or imagine over the internet and have it delivered. One can now get all the news that is and was available on the TV and more.

The point here is that American culture has changed dramatically, and the population of America is strained to keep up with it. The elderly adapt much more slowly, and people tend to become more conservative as they grow older, where young people change quickly and often lead changes in American culture. All of these new trends in America have an impact upon how it feels to be an American and what it feels like to live in American culture. America was humiliated from the year 2000 until the year 2008, having the village idiot as the dictator. The haptic sensory input available in this country has changed dramatically as has the overall experience of being a citizen in America.

In addition to major changes in American culture, the world culture of the planet has also changed.

The global economy is more dependent on American Agribusiness than ever, which is very destructive to the environment.

America is a leader in defining culture globally, as Western culture slowly but surely infects every part of the globe. I call this the creation of a Global American Culture. Even in China one can find Pizza Hut and McDonald's restaurants, as well as American soft drinks like Coca Cola and popular music styled after American pop, which has become increasingly weak in creativity and talent.

As American culture has infected other countries around the world, the world has also fought back. Examples of this include a recent surge in Islamic fundamentalism, a revitalization of traditional values of many nations' cultures, and the development of the internet as a bastion of People Power, perhaps the last one available to citizens of every country.

Male chauvinism still reins over the entire world, and has defenders in every country. This phenomenon I call the World-Wide Testosterone Epidemic. Some of these defenders include Fundamentalists of all stripes, stalkers, rapists, child molesters, and other forms of low-lives, people rampaging for fun and profit, survivalists and right-to-lifers. Some of the forms of discrimination against females are grossly abusive physically and mentally. These sad practices include female genital mutilation and female infanticide.

The world-wide culture has changed dramatically from what it used to be. Because of this it feels completely different to be alive in the world these days than it did in previous decades. As the world changes, so does the experience of being alive in it.

Chapter 12: Summary and Conclusions

There have been many approaches to explaining human behavior, technology, language, art, interpersonal relations and other aspects of human culture over the last hundred years or so by various members of the social sciences community. This book contains my theories as to how the sense of touch is ultimately responsible for how human beings relate to their environment, to one another, and how they develop, manipulate and understand art and technology.

The sense of touch is at the root of every kind of sensory perception that people have. The sense of hearing is the interpretation of the signals coming from the ears responding to vibrations touching the tympanic membrane of the ear. The sense of sight is based on the brain receiving signals from photons (light) touching the light and color sensors (rods and cones) located at the back of the eye. The sense of smell is the result of molecules touching the olfactory nerves in the sinus cavities. Every sense that humans have is based in the sense of touch.

The sense of touch, that is the haptic sense, is responsible for giving human beings the ability to sense and manipulate the environment in such a way as to give them the ability to use their hands to create various forms of technology and art. The development of technology and art is executed by means of algorithms and heuristics which are series of steps used to produce desired goals. The sense of touch makes it possible for people to execute these steps and interpret sensory feedback in order to reach a successful outcome and obtain the desired result. Ultimately, everything created by human culture is the result of the development of technology and/or art, which is only possible through the use of haptic feedback – the sense of touch.

In the past, various approaches to the explanation of human

behavior, while sometimes insightful, are often not comprehensive because they take instinct, the desire to reproduce and/or the desire to obtain power into account, but they tend to overlook the simple and yet powerful sense of touch, without which human existence would be of an entirely different nature. The sense of touch itself guides everything from feeding one's self to interacting with other people. The sense of touch gives people the ability to enjoy food, music, sexual reproduction and the presence of people about whom they care.

It is my hope that by seeing the human experience as a result of the sense of touch, a deeper understanding can be achieved. Because we as humans are living spirits inside of physical bodies, the relationship we have with the environment and other people in the environment is the essence of human existence itself. If we were disembodied spirits floating around in the world like ghosts, the nature of our existence would be entirely different. The fact that we exist in physical bodies is what makes the consideration of the sense of touch indispensable.

Deepak Chopra states that the body and mind are not separate, but that we as living spirits are given a bodymind which is an intimately and totally connected biological tool which we use to evolve and seek enlightenment.

The heart, nervous system and bodymind are connected in such a way that to affect one part of the system affects all other parts as well. If you hurt a person physically, it causes stress to the nervous system and hurts their feelings as well. If a person hurts another person's feelings, it causes the nervous system stress and contributes to psychosomatic illness. Deepak also states that all illness is ultimately a psychosomatic phenomenon, not just obvious diseases like cardiac arrest and ulceration of the stomach.

I have illustrated how all interaction with the environment is the result of the haptic sense. The health of the bodymind is a direct result of the sense of touch as the individual encounters and interacts with other people, situations and objects in their environment. The experiences that one has in life will determine what stresses go into (and come out of) his nervous system, and therefore what kind of person he is. Every interaction a person has with other people has a direct impact on the health of that person's bodymind. The sense of touch is at the root of these personal interactions, and the quality of that touching experience will determine what kind of influence a person has on the people around them.

Regardless of whether an interaction is executed merely verbally, physically or a combination of both, it is still a form of touching between the individuals involved. If you are kind to other people, then you are touching them in a way that is nourishing to their life and their bodymind, which in turn will affect how they interact with other people. If a person is angry and hurtful to others (a Lucy), they will have a negative affect on the bodymind of their victims, and cause an effect that is destructive to life.

On the level of consciousness, we as humans are all interconnected to one another, and it is not possible to touch another person in a hurtful way without damaging one's own nervous system and bodymind in the process.

As anthropologists and sociologists, it is advantageous to take into account the haptic sense in interpreting the development of human technology and human culture, and explaining the behavior of past human cultures as well as those that are in existence in the world today.

As living human beings, it is wise to take into account the fact that every touch you convey to your environment and fellow human beings has a direct impact and affect on who you are. If you hurt yourself, you hurt everybody else as well. Hurting anyone or anything also is destructive to you as an individual, and to the relationship your spirit has with your bodymind.

If you truly wish to evolve and become enlightened, it is a wise path to take to put attention on making every touch you deliver to the world around you and the people in that world one that is nourishing to life and not destructive.

APPENDIX 1: The Haptics of Old Age

One of the less appetizing consequences of old age is the deterioration of the short term memory. This area has generated a substantial amount of research; however, there is little that I am aware of that deals with the decay of our abilities to execute daily algorithms. (But, see the Home Improvements program on the Accessible house.)

In terms of algorithms, this seems to occur in a variety of ways: loss of individual steps, out-of order steps, loss of measures for correcting poorly executed steps, loss of items within a given alternative set, loss of precision in the execution of macros.

Loss of bodily competence figures in here as well; growing weaknesses in the musculature and loss flexibility of the joints add new dimensions of bodily awareness, and call for novel solutions (rewriting of algorithms).

Walking, standing, and bending over become increasingly problematic; gravity becomes a grave concern; the ground becomes The Enemy.

Another of the less pleasant aspects of old age is the deterioration of algorithmic skills which were acquired gradually and painfully during childhood. For men, urinating and defecating are prime examples.

Possibly most important: the gradual loss of gumption, the growing feeling that nothing is worth it any more.

APPENDIX 2: Horace Miner Quote

"The fundamental belief underlying the whole system (of Nacirema culture) appears to be that the human body is ugly and that its natural tendency is to debility and disease. Incarcerated in such a body, Man's only hope is to avert these characteristics through the use of the powerful influences of ritual and ceremony. Every household has one or more shrines devoted to this purpose. The more powerful individuals in the society have several shrines in their houses and in fact, the opulence of a house is often referred to in terms of the number of such ritual centers it possesses. Most houses are of wattle and daub construction, but the shrine rooms of the more wealthy are lined with stone. Poorer families imitate the rich by applying pottery plaques to their shrine walls.

While each family has at least one such shrine, the rituals associated with it are not family ceremonies but are private and secret. The rituals are normally only discussed with children, and then only during the period when they are being initiated into these mysteries. I was able, however, to establish sufficient rapport with the natives to examine these shrines and have the rituals described to me.

The focal point of the shrine is a box or chest which is built into the wall. In this chest are kept the many charms and magical potions without which no native believes he could live. These preparations are secured from a variety of specialized practitioners. The most powerful of these are the medicine men, whose assistance must be rewarded with substantial gifts. However, the medicine men do not provide curative potions for their clients, but decide what the ingredients should be and then write them down in an ancient and secret language. This writing is understood only by the medicine men and by the herbalists who, for another gift, provide the required charm.

The charm is not disposed of after it has served its purpose, but is placed in the charm-box of the family shrine. As these magical materials are specific for certain ills, and the real or imagined maladies of the people are many, the charm-box is usually full to overflowing. The magical packets are so numerous that people forget what their purposes were and fear to use them again. While the natives are very vague on this point, we can only assume that the idea in retaining all the old magical materials is that their presence in the charm-box, before which the body rituals are conducted, will in some way protect the worshipper.

Beneath the charm-box is a small font. Each day every member of the family, in succession, enters the shrine room, bows his head before the shrine box, mingles different sorts of holy water in the font, and proceeds with a brief rite of ablution. The holy waters are secured from the Water Temple of the community, where the priests conduct elaborate ceremonies to make the liquid ritually pure.

In the hierarchy of magical practitioners, and below the medicine men in prestige, are specialists whose designation is best translated as "holy-mouth-men." The Nacirema have an almost pathological horror of and fascination with the mouth, the condition of which is believed to have a supernatural influence on all social relationships. Were it not for these rituals of the mouth, they believe that their teeth would fall out, their gums bleed, their jaws shrink, their friends desert them, and their lovers reject them. They also believe that a strong relationship exists between oral and moral characteristics. For example, there is a ritual ablution of the mouth for children which is supposed to improve their moral fiber.

The daily ritual performed by everyone includes a mouth-rite. Despite the fact that these people are so punctilious about the care of the mouth, this rite involves a practice which strikes the uninitiated stranger as revolting. It was reported to me that the ritual consists of inserting a small bundle of hog hairs into the mouth, along with certain magical powders, and then moving the bundle in a highly formalized series of gestures." (Miner, 1956, 503-507)

Miner, Horace
1956 "Body Ritual among the Nacirema", American Anthropologist, 58:503-507

APPENDIX 3: Why are Humans Hairless?

Anthropologists have speculated that the reason human beings have lost their hair covering a majority of their bodies over the course of evolution is that reading facial expressions is so important that they have a better survival rate when they can communicate non-verbally with greater facility.

I have no doubt that this is the case, but it is likely that another contributing factor is the importance of haptic feedback and communication through touching of other people and features in the environment.

My parents Donald and Patricia Crim also agree that the reason women almost never grow facial hair (or at least, not nearly as much as men) is that it allows mothers to tell the temperature of their baby by pressing their faces against their babies' tummy. A mother with lots of facial hair would not as easily be able to determine whether their baby has a fever. Mothers with little or no facial hair would be able to take steps to cure their babies more quickly than mothers with more facial hair, so it became evolutionarily beneficial for women to not have facial hair in order for their offspring to survive.

GLOSSARY: A HAPTIC LEXICON

The following set of terms have evolved during the past three decades over the breakfast and supper table at our house, and is intended to illustrate a kind of specialized jargon that has developed in order to allow us to talk about our experiences of the world, both inside and outside the individual, in terms of the haptic viewpoint. This is not intended as merely a self-indulgent exercise in family cuteness, although it may strike the reader that way. The tone may seem a trifle smart-ass; however, the intent is serious.

* * * * * * *

ADUMBRATIVE BEHAVIOR: A useful term from Edward Hall, denoting those acts which need to be done before beginning a task. Not to be confused with "preparations", which are the immediate pre-beginning steps. "Adumbrations" are more a matter of deep background, and of choosing appropriate strategies. A chef does preparations for beginning a recipe by assembling the appropriate ingredients and cooking gear. His adumbrations consist of his prior training and experiences which allow him to choose and execute prep algorithms successfully.

AGGRESSIVE SQUID: An interpersonal tactic which consists of attacking suddenly and without warning, and then scuttling behind a screen (or cloud of ink) in order to be protected against counterattack.

ALGORITHM: Any formula consisting of a finite list of components, and a finite series of steps, either linear or ramifying, directed toward producing a desired outcome or result. The Chomskyian Finite State Grammar probably constitutes an instance. Humans are constantly engaged in writing and running algorithms, and in some societies (such as the USA), the successes and failures that people experience at running algorithms become significant sources of self-satisfaction or self-blame, with corresponding gains or losses of gumption. "Murphy's Law" represents a major codification of the frustrations individuals experience when algorithms refuse to run smoothly, or refuse to run at all.

THE "AS-SOON-AS-I": A response to a request or demand to do a certain thing, which is a mild form of refusal. This response may be humorously quantified by the requester, as in, "I'll let you have three 'as-soon-as-I's'".

BACK-LOADING: A common type of occurrence encountered while executing an algorithm, in which one or more preliminary steps become necessary before actually commencing the execution of a chosen algorithm. This is a prime source of gumption-drain. (But, see "side-loading")

BAD CHARACTER: the object of many two-party verbal games is to get the other person to admit to having, not merely bad judgment, but ultimately, bad character. If this is what your opponent is aiming at, you can frustrate his efforts by admitting to bad character at the very beginning of the game, and thus ruining it for him.

BEAUTIFUL EXPERIENCE, A: One of those handy TM folklore terms, used to characterize an event which was entirely lacking in rewards of any kind. It was originally applied to the Great Garbage Explosion.

"BE HONEST WITH YOUR-SELF": A phrase frequently used to admonish the young. "Honesty" has little to do with the case; in haptic terms, the person is being admonished to be critical of his/her own performance, and, above all, not to give him/herself credit for having done something well.

BLISS NINNY: A type of personal matrix encountered on

the MIU campus in Fairfield, Iowa, characterized by being so totally "on the program" that s/he is incapable of normal discourse, or of admitting the possibility that things are not completely rosy. The face is wreathed in a perpetual grin.

BLISS TRAUMA (from Thomas Duncan): A condition of sensory overload brought about by too much bliss (joy, ecstasy, etc.) experienced in too short a time period. This is presumably a pre-condition for the "bliss-ninny" state.

CIVIL INATTENTION: A lovely term from Erving Goffman, which stands for a consensual tactic used by participants in an event. When something sufficiently offensive or embarrassing takes place, the players non-verbally agree to treat this occurrence as a "non- event". This is probably most common in connection with the breaking of wind. (See CRIM'S LAW.)

CODED MESSAGE: Many human messages contain one or more messages inside (or beneath) the overt, surface message. This hidden message is sometimes referred to as the "subtext" (see Goffman, "back-channel"). The hidden message is most commonly of haptic nature, containing a judgment of the receiver as being worthy or unworthy to receive a particular message, or some other sort of haptic judgment or demand.

CRIM'S LAW: Short for "Crim's Law of Social Interaction". Succinctly stated, it goes as follows: "When, during a social gathering, someone sneaks one out, the fattest person present will inevitably be blamed."

DIARRHEA OF THE MOUTH: A tactic in which an individual grabs and holds the floor in a social situation, refusing to relinquish it, and blocking access of other potential talkers. This tactic may arise from more than one set of preconditions, such as amphetamine ingestion, fear of the introduction of a threatening topic, low tolerance of the opinions of others, lack of respect for other players, an intense desire for attention, etc.

DIPSHIT MESSAGE, THE: Any message received by an individual, from any source (another person, organism, or other entity in the environment, or from any internal source), which begins, "Look, Dip-shit ..." Information packaged with a negative haptic message. Frequently comes from God. In its most virulent form, it consists of the negative judgment without any additional information.

"EVERYTHING ON THE FARM EATS MORE AND PRODUCES LESS THAN THE BOOKS TELL YOU." This is a classic quote from Carla Emery's The Old-Fashioned Cook Book; which is also a crystalline statement of a certain pay-off matrix.

FAIRY PRINCESS: another personal matrix, this one designating an individual who expects and demands special privileges, considerations, courtesies, etc. Such a person can be of either gender. Among contemporary USians, this is most commonly found in young, thin, pretty women, the stock from which come beauty contest winners and high fashion models. Culturally, they are defined as winners long before they enter their first contest. There is a down side, however; anorexia and bulimia stalk the ranks of fairy princesses.

FATS: Fat people.

FECAL VALUES: for an unfortunately large number of young males in USian society, these are the values to live by. The two premises are:

1. "I don't take no shit." (Translated into haptic terms, this means that discourtesy or even violence against others is justified, or even admirable, in defense of one's Face.)

2. "I don't give a shit." (Haptic translation: I take no

responsibility for the consequences of my own actions or anyone else's.)

One of the more unfortunate consequences of the Feminist revolution is that young women are now allowed to adopt fecal values.

GASTROPORNOGRAPHY: Scenes or accounts of scenes in which fat people talk about how good food tastes, or, even worse, actually eat. Among contemporary urban middle-class Anglo USians, this is about as serious a social crime as you might commit. The Eating Contest is also a form of gastropornography.

GENDERISM: What is popularly referred to as "sexism"; this is more accurate in that what is usually at issue here is the cultural definitions of sex roles.

GLAMOUR-ORIENTED: A wonderful example of USian trash values: people with this value orientation spend much of their time, resources, and gumption creating a public image of themselves as being willing and even eager to have sex with strangers. Probably no more destructive than addictions to drugs, alcohol, tobacco, or violence and sometimes found is association with one or more of the above.

GUILTY BUTTON: Within the framework of seeing social interaction as haptic exchange, it is assumed that making the other party feel guilty (that is to say, that they owe you a certain kind and number of strokes) is a promising strategy for getting them to do what you want them to do. Once you have convinced them that this is the case, then, in the future, all you have to do is to re-invoke that obligation. This is what is meant by "pushing their guilty button".

GUILTY POINTS: An endeavor to quantify the haptic notion of obligation (see previous definition). The number of guilty points indexes the extent of the other person's obligation to you.

GUMPTION: From Robert Pirsig; a dimension of living and performance which makes it possible to be successful at accomplishing a goal or set of goals. (See GUMPTION RESERVOIR.) In terms of haptics, we fall into gumption traps in the course of running algorithms or executing heuristics.

GUMPTION DRAIN: The process of losing gumption; see GUMPTION TRAPS.

GUMPTION RESERVOIR: in certain instances, gumption may be thought of a having a quantitative dimension. Pirsig's "gumption traps" clearly implies this. Since gumption is gained or lost in the course of daily life, and since most activities required a certain minimum budget of gumption, it follows that there must be an internal reservoir of gumption, which, like pep, can be drawn on at times of high demand, and restocked at times when the demands for expenditure are low, or restocked by rewarding experiences..

GUMPTION TRAPS: another of Pirsig's useful terms, standing for those circumstances which drain one of gumption, and block the achievement of goals. Pirsig's illustrations are taken entirely from motorcycle maintenance; however, examples may be adduced from a much wider variety of cultural algorithm inventories. Pirsig subdivides these into "setbacks" and "hang-ups", and this is certainly a good start; however, I believe that this taxonomy can admit considerable fine-tuning.

HAPTIC: The central concept of this entire argument. It refers to that bundle of sensations generally identified with the sense of touch, but includes sensations internal to the body, as well as external. In its extended sense, it accounts for the human ability to create and manipulate symbols, to perceive and define each other, and to create and manage interpersonal systems of relationship. It also adds a new dimension to the discussion of primate evolution.

HEURISTIC: Any bundle of strategies designed to produce a desired outcome or result. Unlike the algorithm, the heuristic cannot be represented by the formal limitation set given above. Generally, heuristics are larger patterns of organized behavior, and may include more than one actor, and/or devices such as a random number generator which violate the algorithmic requirements of finiteness or sequentiality. Heuristics may contain one or more algorithms, frequently as options or subroutines.

HIGH-PRICE MARKET PLACE, THE: This constitutes a larger context within which human actors deal with each other, in which the penalties for performance errors are sky-high, and in which the actors become motivated to prove each other wrong, to the practical exclusion of other motivations. In the realm of scientific and scholarly discourse, for example, this has become a major motivator for many scholars. Guilty points constitute the principle currency in this market place. This fertilizes a consideration of escalation mechanisms. Examples: the Jewish Momma, ALL soap operas, murder mysteries, science fiction, action films, and fantasy (literary genres).

"HUG-OO, QUEEZE-OO ME": A request by the speaker for a particular physically affectionate response from the listener. Like all baby- talk phrases when used between adults, this one signals that, at least temporarily, the speaker is claiming infant status vis a vis the listener, who thus becomes the nurturing parent. The phrase was actually coined by Dorothy Crim, age 14 months.

INNOCENCE: The state of the human psyche at birth, according to one view, a state in which no stresses have as yet accumulated, and the individual is an original "state of grace". Those who hold to reincarnation as a doctrine have little use for this view. Also, neo-Hobbesians and neo-Freudians find this view too grotesque for words.

JEWISH MOMMA: A personal matrix made famous by at least three generations of Jewish writers and comedians, from Henny Youngman to Phillip Roth. Embodied in a number of supposed quotes from the J.M., such as "Don't bother changing the light-bulb; I'll just sit here in the dark." The essence of this bundle of interpersonal ploys is the manipulation of guilt, combined with the High-Price Market Place.

KISS YOU INTO SUBMISSION: One of the devices by which the marketplace can be lowered is the playful translation of a conventional threat into a non-conventional verbal caress. Originally discovered in an early episode of M*A*S*H. Hawkeye is explaining to a nurse, "If you don't (do this) right now, I may have to kiss you into submission." Like so much early MASH humor, this is extremely sexist (genderist.)

LATERAL THINKING: I originally encountered this term in Pirsig, although it may not have been his coinage. Refers to thinking which takes place outside the conventional structure of thought and discourse. All genuinely original thought, and presumably most if not all psychotic thought, falls into this category.

"LIFE IS LIKE A WELL" STROKE, THE: A type of stroke which occurs most commonly in the context of urban, middle-class USian culture, and more specifically, among education elites. It is based on the assumption that to be right is the supreme reward, and that only one participant in a given situation CAN be right. The phrase itself comes from the story of the searcher who looked the world over for a guru who could explain to him the meaning of life. When he found him (in a cave in Tibet, of course), the guru told him, "life is like a well!" A year later, the searcher returned, to ask the guru what he meant by his statement, to which the guru responded, "So..., maybe life ISN'T like a well!"

Among intellectuals and academics, the quest for this stroke can become an all-absorbing preoccupation, and can even be seen as the major focus in one view of science, the Popperian view. Needless to say, there are other views possible.

LIMITED GOOD: Originally formulated by George Foster to apply to peasant communities, this is a very common assumption found in most, if not all, human societies. The main idea here is a belief that good is limited, and that someone is going to have to go without. Conventional economic theories (both capitalist and Marxist) embrace this assumption. All competitions, economic or not, are based on this assumption. Even competitions in which no limited good is evident arbitrarily define and specify a limited good, as, for example, in Miss America and other beauty contests. In a truly enlightened society, you might search in vain for a "limited good". One key to human happiness is not in unlimited resources, but rather, in reasonably limited wants.

LITTLE-OLD-LADY-IN-A-WHEEL-CHAIR: One member of the inventory of personal matrices generated by this theory; in this instance, the individual who attacks another, and defends her/himself against counterattack by appearing so vulnerable that no responsible person would DREAM of hitting her/him back.

"LOOK AT THE BIRDY": An emblem of that class of utterances designed to steer the conversation away from a stressful topic. This was invented by my mother, Grace Crim, who would actually glance out the window and point at a bird. However, this tactic can be employed regardless of the presence of a window.

LOW-PRICE MARKET PLACE, THE: The opposite of the "high-price market place", this denotes a social framework in which the penalties for performance errors are low, and individual are able to deal with each other in a generally unthreatened manner. Trivial errors are generally ignored (treated with civil inattention), or if not ignored, may be compensated by modest verbal recognition (the "Oops" stroke). What do NOT occur are escalation and scape-goating. Tollison understood the value of the low-price market place when he said, "Don't fix the blame; fix the situation." This gives rise to the consideration of de-escalation mechanisms. Examples include the "OOPS" stroke, the "SKIP THE SMALL SHIT" statement, "It's no big deal", the WIN-WIN situation (Harris),

THE MAD SPACE: In terms of interfamilial haptics, we have observed there is a unique position. The Mad Space, which can be occupied by only one person at a time, at least, in a stable family. In unstable families, individuals contend for the privilege of occupying this space, which lies at the heart of all quarrels and fights. In stable families, people agree to take their turns.

MOMMY LOSES: in most contemporary Anglo, urban, middle-class USian families, this is one of the principal means of acculturating the young. A parallel strategy, DADDY LOSES, is occasionally played, but with a much lower frequency of occurrence. It may be psychically costly for mothers, but is assumed to be correspondingly benign for the children. To persons outside the immediate family, this game appears to lead directly to the spoiling of the child. The label defines the game.

MONOPOLY MONEY: Strokes vary in their authenticity. (Complements are one variety of strokes which illustrate this.) Since all players in social encounters are assumed to be motivated to maximize their returns in authentic good strokes, a tactic for maximizing is to give a high-denomination phony stroke, and demand change in genuine strokes. The analogous situation would be to pay for a diamond ring in Monopoly money, and demand change in real currency.

MOUTH BREATHING: A symptom of low gumption

levels. The individual is inclined to sit, stare at the walls, and mouth-breathe. A possibly more constructive response to this condition would be to engage in gumption-building activities.

ONE, TWO, THREE ...N-HANDED TASKS: Tasks may be usefully classified by the number of hands required simultaneously for successful completion. Much of the technology of the work-shop consists of devices that substitute for one or more of the required hands, such as vices, clamps, and saw-horses. Male work crews occasionally have tasks that require the maximum number of hands available in the crew, but a man doing construction alone might find himself one hand (or more) short to accomplish a given task. The rest of the time, some men work, while others watch and rest. The average crew engaged in street repairs spends approximately 1% of their time in max-hand tasks.

OLD FART AND OLD FARTRESS: Are generally to be observed in the car just ahead, driving ten miles an hour under the speed limit, in the middle lane. She is driving, and he is wearing a fedora (an old-fashioned hat with a brim), and his head is bobbing.

"OOPS" STROKE, THE: A response to one's own trivial miscue, or that of another player in the interpersonal game. This is a way of lowering the market-place, and is characteristic of stable families.

PASSING THE PAIN: We used this term for several years in order to denote the transaction of pain from one person to another. The PAIN DUMPER (Lucy) passes the pain to the PAIN TAKER, who either swallows it (becoming the PAIN BEARER, or Charlie Brown), or passes it on to another party. Within a stratified social system, the vertical status positions may be quantified by enumeration of these pain-based transactions.

PEP: Hardly a technical term, yet it takes on new dimensions when used in contrast with "gumption" (q.v.). It refers simply to physical energy; its creation within the body, and its expenditure in activity. Gumption and pep tend generally to vary together: however, a number of examples will be adduced later which will indicate that this is not always the case.

PERMISSION STROKE, THE: Individuals spend a certain amount of their social time and gumption trying to obtain the permission stroke from another person. Depending on the relative status of the two parties, this may be easy or difficult. On *Cheers*, for example, Cliff (the original STROKE-NEEDER) is frequently engaged in trying to get permission to brag, whether about his recent Florida vacation, his prowess as a stud, his knowledgeability (the LIFE IS LIKE A WELL stroke), or whatever. And since he is generally at the bottom of the informal *Cheers* hierarchy, the others conspire to prevent him from receiving this permission.

PERSONAL MATRIX: A human personality may be characterized as an input - output matrix of haptic messages. Initially formulated to characterize a normal, living human body, it was generalized by our ancient ancestors to other living bodies (animals, birds, fish, plants), to deceased humans (ancestors), and even to inanimate objects, environmental features, weather events, and celestial phenomena. The explication of this definition will require at least two chapters and probably more.

PISSWILLY: Another of those vicious, judgmental personal matrix definitions which adorn this lexicon. This one characterizes the teen-age male who is totally absorbed in defending and protecting his masculine “Face”. In its most virulent form, it is organized around FECAL VALUES (q. v.). Female form: PISSWILLA.

RECREATIONAL PAIN: Pain that is suffered by someone else, someone with whom you enjoy no particular rapport. USians are positively addicted to recreational pain, from professional sports and "action" films to soap operas, which must indicate something about the pain level in this culture.

SELF-STROKER, THE: The major source, if not the only source, of gumption within the individual; we create our initial sense of self from self-exploration in a physical sense, and then, as we acquire the sense of language as haptic exchange, we learn to conduct self- stroking in an internal, verbal manner. It is possible that we continue to engage in self-stroking with subjective haptic messages NOT mediated by silent speech. (N. B., Meditation is PURE self- stroking, with the mantra serving not only as a pleasurable self- stroke, but also as an effective means of "turning off the internal verbalizer", a necessary pre-condition for transcending.) Now, conventional psychological wisdom holds that it is how others treat the individual that produces gumption; this partial truth obscures the significance of self-transactions. Haptic messages received from others are always filtered through the self-stroker, which assigns the appropriate value to them. We always "consider the source" when evaluating messages received from the outside; the more the source individual is valued, the higher the truth value assigned to her/his message, regardless of whether the message is positive or negative. Self-stroking can also be of a physical, sensory or gustatory nature (eating when you feel bad.) Talking to oneself can be a form of self-stoking.

SIDE-LOADING: When in the course of executing an algorithm, you suddenly discover that before completing the task, a long detour (a sequence of additional steps) has become necessary.

SILENTING: Not merely the state of being silent in a social encounter, but rather, the substitution of silence for an expected response. Usually carries a message of hurt feelings, minor irritation, low level of investment in the encounter, etc.

"SKIP THE SMALL SHIT": Another codification of low market-place values. Translated, it would mean, "Don't get hung up on trivia." Richard Farina utilizes it to advantage in his *Been Down So Long It Seems Like Up to Me*.

SMART HANDS: Many authors have noted that verbal and manual intelligence do not always go together. Thus, "smart hands, dumb head" describes a condition frequently encountered, as is its converse, "dumb hands, smart head." James Jones, in *From Here to Eternity*", presents this as the contrast between the Talkers and the Doers.

SNEAKY EATER: at first glance, this one might seem obvious; however, if you didn't grow up in a family with one or more FATS, you would not be able to savor the richness of this phrase. The sneaky eater can drift through a kitchen with barely a pause and absorb at least 500 calories. In addition, the sneaky eater has a shrewd, animal instinct for when the kitchen is unoccupied, and can move in like silent lightning, absorb a vast amount of calories (standing, never sitting), and drift innocently out again, with only barely perceptible moisture on the lips (an example of GASTROPORNOGRAPHY).

STROKE: This useful term comes originally from Eric Berne, and retains some of its utility despite its general trashing by Berne's followers. Our usage differs from Berne in that:

1) Berne limits his use to interpersonal haptic events and messages. Our usage includes all haptic messages directed toward material objects, toward one's own body, received from the interior of one's own body, and/or experienced subjectively within the individual's consciousness.

2) Berne implies strongly that strokes are found principally if not exclusively in the context of "games". Our treatment posits that Berne "games" are patterns of interaction to be found in specific, delimited cultural contexts, and that there are alternative patterns within which haptic exchanges take place. There are other games in addition to the von Neumannian "Zero-Sum Game". (Also, see Harris for the "win-win game".)

STROKE-NEEDER: Another haptic personality type; in this instance, a person with such an intense need for certain types of haptic messages that they devote substantial amounts of time, pep, and gumption to getting them from others. Such persons are generally a burden to those around them. See GLAMOUR-ORIENTATION.

STURGEON'S LAW: "Ninety-five percent of anything is shit." Originally formulated by science fiction author Theodore Sturgeon, it constitutes a classic formulation of the principle of Limited Good.

THERAPY GAME, THE: Psychotherapies of all types may provide the basis of this type of haptic encounter. By definition, the patient is confused and incompetent, while the therapist is clear-thinking and competent. Most therapists, and some patients, appear to become addicted to the game, because it presumably provides them with the haptic payoffs which they want or need.

THERAPY JUNKY: An individual who is so addicted to the Therapy Game that they continually missionize, and try to recruit others. For example, a woman explained the other day that she was having a complete psychiatric evaluation done of her youngest child, not because the child appeared to be having any problems, but rather because she had had similar evaluations done on her other two children, and she didn't want the youngest child to "feel left out"!

TIN EAR: Originally referring to individuals with a defective sense of pitch, and now generalized to characterize individuals who lack normal sensitivity, in any of the sensory channels, or expected social skills, and as a consequence, fail to act appropriately in social situations.

TOO-HIGH STARTING PLATFORM, THE: (awkward, but I haven't found a more felicitous substitute) A strategy for structuring competitive events in such a way as to either, a) disqualify most of the competitors at the outset, or b) single out an individual competitor for special humiliation and/or abuse. A particular favorite of public school physical education instructors who, dreaming of coaching future All-Americans, see most of their students as miserable physical specimens. ("Any of you slobs can do at least five push-ups!") USian culture is characterized by an unusual devotion to this strategy. ILLUSTRATION: Sam: "Hey, Norm, how's life in the fast lane?" Norm: "I dunno, I'm still lookin' for the on-ramp."

UMCA: United States Male Caucasian Anglo.

UNANNOUNCED CONTEST, THE: You will recognize yourself as being victimized by this dishonest interpersonal tactic when someone tells you simultaneously that 1) you and s/he have just been in a contest, and 2) you are the loser. This is frequently encountered among Anglo, urban, middle- class women. It is also an excellent technique for collecting gumption from another.

UNSTRESSING: Despite our best efforts to keep TM

jargon to a minimum, we are forced to include this useful term. In its original framework, it referred to the release of stress initially experienced during the practice of Transcendental Meditation, and subsequently outside of meditation. A more general usage has emerged, applying the term to any instance in which an individual is acting inappropriately, under the influence of a powerful emotion. We have determined that stresses may either be released or recycled, although it may be very difficult to determine which is actually taking place in a given situation.

UNSTRESSING YOUR BRAINS OUT: An extreme, though rarely fatal, form of "unstressing" (q. v.). Subjectively, you feel like killing someone, except that it would be just too much trouble.

THE "WAS GUNNA": A temporizing response to a request, or a question as to why a certain task was not performed, as in, "I was gunna do it in the morning." Can also be humorously quantified, like the "as-soon-as-I".

"WHEN THE BUZZARDS COME FLAPPING HOME TO ROOST": An intensification of the idiom, "when the pigeons come home to roost". The intensification is achieved by 1) substituting buzzards for pigeons, and 2) adding "flapping", which seems more ominous than just "come" alone. The implication is that, in addition to flapping home to roost, the buzzards are planning to feed after they arrive.

WHINING INFANT: A largely self-defining term. One can be of any age or gender. The pose of helplessness is hopefully transformable into a legitimate claim to privilege. See LITLE-OLD-LADY-IN-A-WHEELCHAIR.

WORD SALAD: A conversational tactic in which the speaker produces discourse which, while superficially coherent, fails to make overall sense. Generally a defensive tactic, employed when the speaker is afraid he/she will be challenged on some point. There are degrees of "word-saladry".

WORDSMITH: A haptically defined personal matrix. In contrast to all those who labor skillfully with their hands (blacksmiths, coppersmiths, etc.) a wordsmith labors with presumably some skill with the mouth (or the word-processor).

"WOW" STROKE, THE: A high-denomination counter in interpersonal interaction. In eliciting a "wow" stroke, you have induced the other person to admit that they are TOTALLY impressed by what you are doing or saying.

SOURCES CITED

Bateson, Gregory
1972 Steps to an Ecology of Mind, Ballantine Books, New York

Birdwhistell, Ray M.
1970 Kinesics and Context, University of Pennsylvania Press, Philadelphia

Casson, Ronald
1983 "Schemata in Cognitive Anthropology", Annual Review of Anthropology, Vol. 12

Goffman, Erving
1959 The Presentation of Self in Everyday Life, Doubleday, New York

Hall, Edward
1964 "Adumbration as a Feature of Intercultural Communication", American Anthropologist, 66 (6, pt.2), December 1964

Harris, Marvin
1964 The Nature of Cultural Things, Random House, New York
1968 The Rise of Anthropological Theory
1979 Cultural Materialism

Linton, Ralph
1936 The Study of Man, Appleton-Century-Crofts, New York

Lomax, Alan
1976 Cantometrics: A Method in Musical Anthropology, University of California Extension Media Center, Berkeley

Miner, Horace
1956 "Body Ritual Among the Nacirema", American Anthropologist 58: 503-507

Pirsig, Robert M.
1974 Zen and the Art of Motorcycle Maintenance: An Inquiry Into Values, William Morrow, New York (pagination from Bantam edition)

www.ingramcontent.com/pod-product-compliance
Lightning Source LLC
LaVergne TN
LVHW020633100826
845148LV00012B/2165